NATIVE AMERICANS

500 YEARS AFTER

NATIVE AMERICANS

500 YEARS AFTER

photographs by Joseph C. Farber

text by Michael Dorris

THOMAS Y. CROWELL COMPANY
Established 1834
New York

DESIGNED BY JUDITH WORACEK

MANUFACTURED IN THE UNITED STATES OF AMERICA

2-76 BT 1495

LIBRARY OF CONGRESS CATALOGING IN PUBLICATION DATA

Farber, Joseph C   1903–
    Native Americans: 500 years after.

    Bibliography: p.
    Includes index.
    1. Indians of North America—Pictorial works.
I. Dorris, Michael. II. Title.
E77.5.F37 1975   779.9'9730497   75-15994
ISBN 0-690-00728-0

1   2   3   4   5   6   7   8   9   10

Proper acknowledgment for all of the help that I have received while making the photographs for this book would require another volume.

Several people were encouraging from the inception of the project. Among them were Frederick Dockstader, an Oneida and director of the Museum of the American Indian; Oren Lyons, a chief of the Onandaga tribe; William Byler and Arlene Hirschfelder, of the Association on American Indian Affairs; Alphonse Ortiz, a Tewa and professor of anthropology at the University of New Mexico; N. Scott Momaday, a Kiowa and professor of English literature at Leland Stanford University; and Rosebud Yellow Robe, a Sioux.

While working in Alaska I became acquainted with Michael Dorris, a Modoc and the author of this book. He was doing research for a doctoral thesis at Yale University. His understanding and personal contact with large numbers of Native Americans throughout America made him an enjoyable and invaluable collaborator.

As the work went on assistance came from Ira Isham of Nett Lake; James Houston; Alvin Josephy; Phileo Nash; William C. Sturtevant; Webster Two Hawk, a Sioux; Ellen Lang of Native Alaskan Brotherhood; Al Bridges; Hank Adams; Floyd Durham; William Keeler, an Osage; R. C. Gorman, a Navajo; Fritz Scholder, a Mission; Joe Dann Osceola and Fred Smith, Seminoles; Buffalo Tiger, a Miccosukee; Lloyd New, a Cherokee; Clyde Bellecourt and Dennis Banks of AIM; and Sister John André.

Organizing the work was made possible by the great ability of Nicholas Ellison, editor, and the imagination of Judith Woracek, art director.

—*Joseph C. Farber*

CONTENTS

"We only ask an even chance to live as other men live. We ask to be recognized as men. We ask that the same law shall work alike on all men. . . . Let me be a free man—free to travel, free to stop, free to work, free to trade where I choose, free to choose my own teachers free to follow the religion of my fathers, free to think and talk and act for myself—and I will obey every law, or submit to the penalty."

—*Chief Joseph*
(NEZ PERCÉ)

"But it is now time for a destructive order to be reversed, and it is well to inform other races that the aboriginal culture of America was not devoid of beauty. Furthermore, in denying the Indian his ancestral rights and heritages the white race is but robbing itself. But America can be revived, rejuvenated, by recognizing a Native school of thought."

—*Chief Standing Bear*
(SIOUX)

"The mission of photography is to explain man to man and each man to himself."

—*Edward Steichen*
DIRECTOR OF THE DEPARTMENT OF PHOTOGRAPHY
The Museum of Modern Art, 1947–1962
DIRECTOR EMERITUS, 1962–1973

NATIVE AMERICANS

500 YEARS AFTER

0   200
KILOMETERS

UNITED STATES

- Town or city with sizeable Indian population
- Federal Indian reservation

More detailed maps of each division begin each section.

0   200 KILOMETERS

0   200 MILES

A HISTORY

When "in fourteen hundred and ninety-two Columbus sailed the ocean blue," he made an important discovery: not, as he had hoped, an alternate route to the Asian Indies, but instead an alternate route to the Americas. The original channel of discovery and colonization, the Bering land bridge, had, many thousands of years previously, fallen the victim of flood, thus leaving the continent's original inhabitants isolated from the rest of the world and free to increase, develop, and expand independent of any influence other than the dictates of environment and their own individual imaginations.

The original inhabitants of the Americas were a diverse, heterogeneous group of people. They arrived not as a single wing of migration, but in small groups chronologically separated from each other by as much as at least twelve thousand years. They spoke not a single language nor even related languages, but rather their languages derived from well over ten language families, each in magnitude, distinctiveness, and complexity on a par with Indo-European. As a group their cultures shared no common denominator; the society developed by Native People in California had no more, and probably less, in common with that of groups in Michigan than it did with a culture in Polynesia or Spain. There were, in the Americas, as many ethnic groups as there were cultures, as many cultures as there were languages, and the Americas were linguistically among the most diverse areas in the world. In the territory north of the Rio Grande alone at least four hundred separate, distinct, and mutually unintelligible languages were spoken, and at least as many separate societies flourished.

This is not to say, of course, that contact and trade did not exist between many groups or tribes. Modern archeology testifies that networks for the exchange of manufactured and natural products existed throughout both continents. However, no single tribe or group was aware of more than a small fraction of the other extant indigenous societies. A thousand years ago a Hopi was as likely to have heard of a Choctaw as he was to have heard of a Bulgarian, and if he had met a representative from each of the two groups he would probably have considered himself to be equally distinct from and superior to both.

There was, however, an awareness of ethnic plurality in the Americas. Members of any and every group knew of other societies in which people looked, dressed, worshipped, spoke, and acted differently. The diversity of human society was an accepted, expected fact of life and considered to be the normal state of affairs.

As a result of this common attitude, the cultural history of northern America (and henceforth in this essay remarks will be limited to this area) differed in a number of significant respects from that in Europe, Asia, or Africa. Few if any American societies sought to impose either their ideological or political systems on other cultures. While there were a number of multitribal alliances (e.g., Iroquoian, Creek, Huron, Siouian), there were no empires analogous to those of Rome, Persia, or China; there were many travelers and traders but few cultural or religious missionaries. The freedom of the individual almost always predominated over the power of the state. Leadership most usually derived from expertise or proven ability rather than dynastic heredity, and armed conflict between societies depended almost universally upon collective individual choice rather than the orders of a single ruler. With a total population never in excess of about twenty million for all of America north of the Rio Grande there was room enough for difference, and destiny was thought to manifest itself on an individual rather than a societal plane.

While no attitude or aspect of culture could be said to apply universally throughout Native America, two concepts were widely, if unconsciously, shared. The first had to do with the land itself: Most Native American societies considered land to be a commodity similar in kind to air or water or fire—something necessary for human survival but something above personal ownership. Certainly the idea of an individual's right to *use* of a certain piece of property was widespread, but few tribes ascribed absolute *title;* land was "owned" collectively by all who used or inhabited it. When they ceased to use it, it reverted to common availability.

The other generally shared concept concerned the practice of warfare. Armed conflict could occur between tribes, parts of tribes, or individuals for a variety of reasons, but usually the hostilities lasted no longer than a single season, and loss of life was minimal. As a rule there was no insistence upon "total victory" or the complete annihilation of an enemy. Battles were fought for personal reasons—of revenge, honor, or acquisition of property—and once these limited objectives had been achieved the reason for a continued military action no longer existed. Most tribes, of course, had their traditional allies and opponents, but it was indeed a rare conflict in North America which would deprive an enemy of its land or wipe out an opponent entirely.

In the years immediately preceding the beginnings of intensive culture contact wiith Europe, North American societies were dynamic and growing. Athapaskan peoples from the Subarctic had begun to move southward, encountering Eskimo, Cree, and Pueblo opposition; in the east, the newly reconstituted League of the Iroquois had begun a slow shift to the northeast, filling the territorial void left by the declining Huron Confederacy. The urban "Mound Builders" farmed intensively to support cities ranging from Mexico to Maine and sometimes containing populations in excess of ten thousand people. No single tribe or alliance dominated the whole continent, and the vast majority of Native American people lived in small, independent, endogamous societies.

In all probability the first Europeans who came to the Americas were infinitely more surprised to meet Native Americans than Native Americans were to see them. Europeans of the fifteenth century lived in a cultural milieu which was, in comparison with other areas of the world, homogenous. Almost all Europeans spoke languages derived from an Indo-European base, and virtually all of them professed religions stemming from a Judeo-Christian heritage. Though there had been some contact with Africans and Asians, the average European probably had never encountered anyone with a substantially different world view from his own, and common understandings of government, protocol, and dress prevailed from Russia to Portugal. The first Spanish explorers were so taken aback at the very existence of Native Americans that it took a century-long debate involving university scholars and the pope himself before they could accept even the humanity of these peoples.

Native Americans, on the other hand, were quite used to cultural diversity and consequently probably regarded Europeans as no more or less bizarre than any number of tribes other than their own. In all likelihood, the first Native Americans to view Europeans were impressed both by the technology Europeans displayed and by their seeming inability to provide adequate food and shelter for themselves.

It certainly seems clear from the historical evidence that Native Americans, be they in Florida, Massachusetts, Alaska, or New Mexico, were initially quite unafraid of their European visitors and did not foresee that their presence boded ill for the continued stability of Native societies. Rather, the strangers were treated as guests, as trading partners, and, to a certain extent, as curiosities.

For their part, most Europeans apparently didn't know what to think. To their horror and dismay they found that their "New World" was thoroughly inhabited by people who not only did not *understand* long-standing European mores of political, social, and religious behavior, but seemed downright uninterested in these conventions. This attitude, this reluctance to accept a European, any European, as arbiter of truth, beauty, and justice, was imminently threatening to people who had themselves by and large been considered radicals and oddballs, and it was soon given a name: "savage." "Savage," together with its correlatives "primitive" and "heathen," can be defined only in the negative. A savage *isn't* Christian, doesn't wear proper European clothes, doesn't live in a town house, doesn't speak the King's English (or French or Spanish or Russian or Swedish or Dutch), doesn't appreciate the right art or music, isn't white. A savage might be *noble*, but he certainly isn't equal. And everyone knew what GOD would do if given a choice between backing a civilized European or a savage Native American. . . .

Those first Europeans, and perhaps even a majority of their descendents, made one more key negative generalization which they called "Indian." What, after all, *is* an Indian? Not, certainly, a European. Not an African or an Asian. But . . . "a child of the forest," a "heathen devil," "pesty," drunk, inappropriate. An "Indian" quite simply was, and for many non–Native Americans still is, a nonwhite, nonblack aboriginal inhabitant of North or South America. It's simply another way of saying THEM, and just about as explanatory. And with this generalization a new, artificial, and completely invalid ethnic group emerged upon the world scene, the product of a myopic European imagination: The INDIAN was born.

Of course nobody realized the "Indians" were "Indians" except Europeans. Cherokees still thought they were Cherokees, Mohawks and Cree thought they could still tell each other apart, and Mandans foolishly went on being Mandans. But what did it matter? After all, they were all only INDIANS, and what did INDIANS know?

This new category made it infinitely more simple for Europeans to deal with the various peoples they "discovered." If you lost a fight with one "Indian" you could take your revenge on any other "Indian" you happened upon, no matter what tribe he thought he was. Any "Indian" could make a quick land deal for any tribe. The transgressions of an individual "Indian" became immediately a racial trait. And finally and inevitably this broad misunderstanding reached its ultimate conclusion: "The only good Indian is a dead Indian."

This categorical lumping was particularly inappropriate when applied to a population which took great pride in tribal and individual distinctions. Native Americans suffered all the negative effects of the generalization without benefiting from any of its potentially positive implications. Europeans, assuming that all "Indians" were not only alike but telepathic as well, projected each conflict with an individual band or tribe into a forthcoming Great Indian Alliance, dedicated to pushing the hapless Europeans into the sea.

They thereby rationalized untold numbers of "retaliatory" actions against basically peaceful Natives as simply self-preservation. The epitome of this hysteria came when less than a hundred starving Modocs, holding out in a box canyon in Oregon in the late nineteenth century, prompted scare headlines in newspapers from St. Louis to Philadelphia.

While it is true that on occasion a common need would force disparate tribes into a temporary alliance—one remembers Pontiac, Black Hawk, Tecumseh and Sitting Bull—in reality for the most part Native American people were divided into a multiplicity of small bands as mistrustful of each others' motivations as they were of those of Europeans or white Americans. Barring a miracle, there was no way after about 1650 that the European immigrants could be significantly dislodged or persuaded by force from doing anything they pleased.

For all the fanfare, relatively few people on either side lost their lives in the various "Indian wars." Far fewer, in fact, than one might expect it would take to dispossess ten million people from a continent they had inhabited and controlled for at least forty thousand years.

Much more significant than battles or massacres are two factors which paved the way for European dominance over North America: disease and the treaty.

The Native population of North America declined, between 1492 and 1910, from something in excess of ten to fifteen million people to a government estimate of two hundred and ten thousand. Only a tiny percentage of this loss can be ascribed to assimilation; an even smaller number died in battle or massacre; and only a few hundred Native Americans migrated from the United States to Canada or Mexico. The remainder of the people—million upon million of them—died of plague and disease carried to the Americas by Europeans.

Archeology, folklore, and recorded history all suggest that the contiguous continents of Europe, Asia, and Africa had been, over the past many thousand years, swept periodically by maladies which decimated large segments of human population. Native Americans, "out of touch" with inhabitants of other areas of the world for at least ten thousand years, had never experienced the waves of smallpox, typhus, measles, tuberculosis, and syphilis which affected the "Old World." Therefore they had no knowledge of these diseases and their medicine had developed no means for their prevention or cure.

Genetic mutation naturally preadapts some percentage of a large enough population to be more resistant to a given illness than the majority. Each time an epidemic appeared in Eurasia or Africa, therefore, those people—often the majority of the population—who had no such "natural immunity" died. The survivors consisted solely of those individuals who were naturally resistant to the disease, and they in turn passed on their ability to survive to their descendents. Over time this resistance became predominant in the population, and while some people might fall prey to one of these diseases, it became increasingly unlikely that virtually an entire population would succumb.

At the same time, European, Asian, and African science and medicine became more effective in dealing with known diseases and preventive steps were taken to decrease the likelihood of a spreading infection.

Without the dubious benefit of this experience, Native Americans were helpless in the face of the myriad diseases which European explorers, missionaries, and later colonists unconsciously carried. Within a mere four hundred years, they experienced the effects of diseases whose appearance had spread and decimated populations in the Old World over many millennia. The result was predictably drastic: Some tribes lost five-sixths to nine-tenths of their total population within a period of weeks when a variety of illnesses infected the group. Often European disease preceded direct contact with Europeans; rather, it was carried to an interior tribe by an infected member of a tribe with whom contact had been made. Whole peoples may indeed have died without ever knowing the nature or source of their ailment.

This lack of natural immunity made Native Americans notoriously bad slaves (few survived long enough to be profitable). Furthermore it placed a most effective weapon in the hands of some nineteenth-century American military personnel who were known to have distributed as trade items blankets which were infected with smallpox. It is impossible to calculate with any probability what percentage of Native American people died "by accident" and what percentage were murdered by intent through the use of germ warfare. In any case, the effect was the same: The Native population was dramatically and almost instantly reduced; societies were torn apart; and the New World daily became at once both emptier and thereby more available to exploitation and colonization. Such is the meaning behind that oft-used and little-understood term "The Vanishing American." One might conclude from reading some American history texts that Natives were simply assumed, lemming-like, into some sort of primeval "happy hunting ground" in order *not* to be in the way of Manifest Destiny. But in fact, in order to provide an analogy to the experience of Native America, the contemporary United States population of 200,000,000 would have to be reduced, by the year 2375, to only 2,800,000 people—about the size of Greater Cleveland. Native America could not at the same time maintain itself in the face of such disaster *and* resist an ever-increasing invading force. Little wonder.

Lethal though contact proved to be for much of the Native population, a substantial number of survivors remained. Europeans, initially small in number and dependent upon the good will and cooperation of New World residents for their own survival, were faced with the task of establishing ongoing working relationships with many tribes. The established *modus operandi* of international European affairs was the treaty. Such an agreement implied a parity between the two or several signatory nations and further established a mutual recognition of the very right of existence.

In dealing with Native American people, Europeans explicitly admitted an all-important concept: the aboriginal right of title to land. Treaties demonstrated that Native Americans not only occupied territory but *owned* it and thus could sell, negotiate, or otherwise profit from land which was theirs, not because it was so stated in a deed but because they and their progenitors had occupied it from "time immemorial."

There would of course seem to be some inconsistency between the dual concepts of "discovery" (as in "I claim this land for ————") and "title," but this paradox seldom interfered with immediate concerns. When a tribe was small or powerless it was "discovered." When it was large and strong it was treated as a nation state. In Europe one country seldom "discovered" another, though treaties occasionally defined nations or ethnic groups out of existence. The treaty system therefore implied a complex set of recognitions, and established the precedent that, even in European eyes, Native Americans lived in internationally recognized states and controlled their own territory.

From the Native point of view the entire system must have seemed bizarre, to say the least. The whole concept of "title" was foreign and, though interesting and profitable, hardly a traditional concern. If no individual or group owned land absolutely, then no other individual or group could buy it and thereafter "own" it. Many of the original treaties would seem to be classic examples of cultural misunderstanding. From the European point of view, Native nations were possessed of a fabulously valuable asset—land—which they seemed willing to part with for unbelievably little recompense (the proverbial $24 worth of beads and trinkets); what poor business people they must have seemed!

From the Native point of view, on the other hand, Europeans seemed maniacally anxious to pay exotic baubles for something which could be neither owned nor sold. (Imagine encountering a gullible foreigner on the street tomorrow who positively insists on paying you $75 for the Brooklyn Bridge.) What poor business people *they* must have seemed! Each side in all probability got a good laugh at putting one over on the other. What a rude awakening it must have been for those shrewd Native con-men when Europeans began to enforce the agreements as they understood them. It must have seemed like a situation in which one person "buys" $5 of air from another and then suddenly says "Stop breathing my air!!!"

Native-European land dealings were complicated by yet a further misunderstanding. In the vast majority of Native American societies, no one individual could speak for another unless that right had been specifically granted. The power of a chief derived from experience and the ability to persuade others—for in general there was no enforcing authority behind the office. Therefore, while an individual Native might be convinced to sell or exchange his *own* rights to a piece of territory, he or she could rarely negotiate for another's land. It was inconceivable, and tantamount to accepting payment today from an insistent would-be buyer of a third party's property.

Europeans initially understood neither this philosophy of ownership nor the complexities of Native American politics and so assumed that each tribe or nation had a leader who, by the very nature of the office, was empowered to treat for all territory occupied by his people. As a result, negotiations were carried on and payments were made to individuals who had no authority over the vast territories in question. When others in the tribe objected, quite logically, that *they* had certainly made no agreement to relinquish their land and therefore did not consider themselves bound by contract, they were often treated as criminals, "Indian givers," and cheats. As always, European military technology settled the question.

As years passed, one might logically conclude that Europeans began to comprehend the subtleties of these misunderstandings. They had, after all, a cumulative experience and continuity in their relations with various Native people.

Treaties were made and broken from the European and later American side with such regularity that it would take virtually a leap of faith to believe that white government officials looked upon treaty making as more than a temporary holding action, easily undone when ever necessary.

The Native perspective, however, was substantially different. The bitter learning experiences of East Coast tribes were by and large unknown by Plains and Western Native Americans. Each tribe or region had perforce to run the gamut of reactions to contact with Europeans—from initial hospitality and credulity to eventual frustration and cynicism. From one perspective it appears that North America was purchased legally, bit by bit. From another it would seem that the continent was stolen by conscious, malevolent intent, by governments preying upon cultural misunderstandings, disease, and powerlessness.

While many treaties were written to apply in perpetuity ("as long as the rivers run and the grasses grow"), historical retrospect suggests that in fact they were intended as a mere transitionary stage until such time as the Native "disappeared." The concept of the Native as "Vanishing American" had been hopefully promulgated for a good three hundred years. Ever since the seventeenth century, tome after scholarly tome had direly predicted the demise of the Indian "within one or two generations at most." Certainly the literature of the nineteenth century suggests that it was widely anticipated that life on a reservation was merely a launching pad to ethnic and cultural oblivion. To the unending consternation of many, however, Native Americans refused to cooperate and stubbornly stayed put.

By the late nineteenth century, virtually all surviving Native Americans were confined to reservations. Conditions were abominable, treaty promises went unkept, Indian agents got rich, and missionaries successfully lobbied a federal ban on the practice of "heathen religions." And yet the melting pot seemed to hold few attractions for Indian people. Instead they seemed more interested in preserving, maintaining, and developing the traditions, languages, and priorities of their own histories.

For four hundred years, Europeans and later white Americans had been hoping, waiting for, and encouraging the original inhabitants of what is now the United States to disappear. Only their nonexistence would validate the myth of the New World and permit the total glorification of America's pioneer past. As long as they remained they constituted contrary evidence to what many Americans would like to believe was the purity, honesty, and nobility of their own history. Native Americans were proof of the self-interest, racism, dishonesty, and intolerance which characterize much of this nation's past.

Removal, or eviction, a tactic employed throughout contact, was apparently a more palatable solution than total genocide. As long as a Native American didn't live near one's own precinct, one could relegate all Indian people to the dim corridors of ancient history and forget them *and* their view of American history. Such was the intent of the Indian Removal Act of the early nineteenth century, which ordered the eviction of almost all Native people east of the Mississippi into lands to the west. As with all such dictates, some American leaders rationalized that their land grab was in the "best interest" of the Natives concerned, since it would "protect" them from the deleterious effects of contact. In fact, it dispossessed peoples, such as the Cherokee, who had already made a stunning and rapid cultural response to the Euro-American presence. Within only a few generations, they had developed a syllabary alphabet and national literacy and had sent many of their young people to study in American universities. They had won a Supreme Court battle establishing the legal definition for a reservation as a sovereign, dependent nation—a ruling whose implications are still strongly felt today. They had allied themselves with the fledgling colonies in both the War of Independence and the War of 1812, and their allegiance may well be responsible for the survival of independence in more than one of the southern states. For their efforts they had been promised full statehood within the Union. Instead they were dispossessed, sent on the infamous Trail of Tears to Indian Territory in Oklahoma. During this forced march in midwinter four of the seventeen thousand of their number perished. But Cherokee land, farms, and crops were grabbed by "homesteaders" in Georgia, the Carolinas, and Tennessee, and that was the whole point in any case.

Throughout the period of cultural contact between Native American peoples and the United States government, education was employed as a means of deculturation. The mission and federal boarding schools which Native youth were required to attend were aimed at achieving primarily social rather than purely academic goals. They enforced Euro-American "Christian" values: the exclusive speaking of English, the work ethic, clock-time orientation, and the like. Children were intentionally incarcerated far from the influence of parents and tribe and called upon to denigrate their own people's history and beliefs. The regimen to which they were subjected most insufficiently prepared them to compete with non-Natives in any skilled area and at the same time kept them from acquiring the practical knowledge necessary for adult life in an Indian community. The intent of the system can only be described as a ruthless attempt to educate them *away* from their own people, and yet they were not educated for any realistic position in white society. Against all odds, however, the vast majority of these Native American children did not in fact reject their origins, but returned home at the earliest opportunity, often to become the most ardent rejectors of an assimilationist position.

Since neither the imprisonment of adults nor the kidnapping of children seemed to effect the disappearance of Native Americans, Congress decided in 1887 to take even more drastic steps. Under the provisions of the General Allotment Act (or Dawes Act), reservation lands owned collectively by tribes were divided "in severalty." Treaties were unilaterally breached and remaining Native-controlled land was divided into small plots, 160 acres or less. The intent of forcing tribal peoples to accept the Euro-American concept of individual land ownership was to speed assimilation by crippling tribal solidarity and influence. Again, this was done in a stated attitude of benevolent paternalism—the Great White Father was educating the Children of the Forest once more.

The immediate result, however, was the forced cession of 60 million of the remaining 138 million acres of Indian land which the government ruled "excess." During the fifty years following allotment, an additional 30 million acres were sold, stolen, or ceded. Native Americans' holdings had been reduced from all of North America in 1492 to 138 million acres in 1887 to 48 million acres in 1934, and all for their own good!

The Dawes Act, which promised to improve the lot of Native Americans, instead saw a drastic decline in the health, education, and welfare of Indian people throughout the country. It benefited only non-Indians—probably to the surprise of few.

MODERN HISTORY

The turn of the twentieth century was an unhappy time for the Native people of America. Their total population was at its lowest ebb, the vast majority of their land had been taken away, their religions were outlawed, their children removed from home and incarcerated in hostile institutions where it was deemed a crime to so much as speak in one's own language. In 1900 few Native Americans were citizens and as a group they constituted the poorest, unhealthiest, and least likely to survive—much less succeed—population in all of the United States. And yet they not only survived, but they survived as a culturally intact group of peoples; against all odds, tribes maintained their languages and wisdom, guarded their art and music and literature, and for the most part, chose to continue to be Indians rather than assimilate and disappear.

The United States government, however, continued to advocate a melting-pot policy, and in 1924 Congress passed the Curtis Act, which conferred American citizenship on all native-born Indians. In many areas, such a change in status did not mean automatic access to the ballot box, however, and Native "citizens" remained disenfranchised "persons under guardianship" in Arizona and New Mexico until 1948.

Nevertheless, citizenship did, in the minds of some congressmen and others, abrogate the rights to special status which were guaranteed through treaty. Questions like "How can we have treaties with our own citizens?" (with its correlative answer: "We can't, therefore throw out the treaties and open up the land!!") should have been asked and answered before any such act was passed. *If it had been made clear that United States citizenship meant abandonment of Native American identity, and *if* the opinion of Native American people had been solicited, it is improbable that even a significant minority of Indian people would have opted for it in 1924.

In effect, the Curtis Act was tantamount to the American government deciding to celebrate the Bicentennial in 1976 by unilaterally declaring all inhabitants of the Western Hemisphere "American citizens" and then immediately forcing any (former) Brazilian, Canadian, or Venezuelan engaging in international trade to comply with United States tariff restrictions and oil prices. Such an expanded Monroe Doctrine precludes all argument. The American experiment with instant naturalization is not unique: The Portuguese tried it in Angola, the Belgians in Zaire, and the French in Algeria—but somehow most Africans apparently never *felt* like Europeans. Most Native Americans didn't either, but by the twentieth century they lacked the population or resources to successfully dispute the denial of their sovereignty.

Four years later, a blue-ribbon congressional committee chaired by Lewis Meriam issued a report on conditions in Indian country. Its aim was to assess the effects of the Dawes and Curtis acts and to inform the government of the progress these pieces of legislation had made possible for Native American people. The situation on reservations in 1928, however, yielded little in the way of optimistic forecast. Since 1887 conditions had universally worsened: The educational level was in most cases lower, the poverty greater, the death rate higher (and for younger people) than at any time previous to the enactment of the "benevolent" policies. Federal enforcement of the misguided and totally unjust severalty laws was, in effect, cultural genocide.

In 1934 President Roosevelt appointed the anthropologist John Collier as Commissioner of Indian Affairs. Unlike too many of his predecessors in office, Collier actually knew something of at least one

Native society (Pueblo) and had long opposed the Allotment policy both for its inhumanity and its naiveté. His major achievement was to assist in the development and passage of the Indian Reorganization Act (the Wheeler-Howard Act), a policy which sought to undo most of the provisions of the Dawes Act and begin to remedy the disasters recounted in the Meriam Report of 1928.

Almost half a century, however, was a long time, and it was beyond realistic possibility that either the land base or the cultural, educational, and economic health of Native American societies could be restored as they were in 1880.

The Wheeler-Howard Act aimed to revive the traditional "bilateral, contractual relationship between the government and the tribes." Commissioner Collier emphasized the Native American right to a kind of self-determination and banned any further allotment of tribal land. The Indian Reorganization Act further authorized severely limited appropriations to purchase new holdings and reclaim certain lost property; it also established a federal loan policy for Native groups and reaffirmed the concept of self-government on reservations.

Many tribes opposed this legislation, however, on the basis of the restrictions and regulations it placed on the participating tribes. The act, for instance, prohibited any individual transfer of tribal land without governmental approval, and it required that all tribal governments conform to a single political system based on majority rule. No tribe was eligible for a single benefit of the act unless it agreed to it *in toto*, and therefore its acceptance necessarily became widespread.

The period following the Collier administration and extending into the early 1950's was one in which many Americans seemed to forget about Indians and assumed that *at last* "they" had finally vanished as predicted. The national interest was focused on World War II and the Korean War, and domestic treaties seemed a thing of the far-distant past.

After one of these "dormant cycles," the public and its government usually seem particularly piqued and frustrated to discover that Native Americans are still very much alive and intact. Once again in the 1950's, as in the 1880's, the presumptuous and thoroughly invalid assumption was made that if Indians had not chosen to disappear into the melting pot, something sinister was to blame. It seems never to have occurred to those in power that Crows or Yakimas, for instance, simply preferred being Crows or Yakimas!

As usual, the federal government, liberal "friends of the Indian," and rural land developers concluded that special status, and the reservation system in particular, were somehow retarding Native assimilation, and therefore it was decided, once again, to breach all legal precepts of international and United States law and unilaterally break treaty agreements. It was further concluded that if some Native Americans insisted that they didn't want to change their relationship with the government, they simply didn't know what was good for them. The rivers were still running, the grass was still growing, but the promises made by the American government and written to apply in perpetuity could not exist for even a century without twice being violated.

A committee was therefore appointed to divide, like Gaul, all reservations into three parts: the "prosperous," the "marginal," and the "poor." Even with this license, only a handful of tribes could be found to fit, by any stretch of the imagination, into the first category, and these were marked for quick termination. The implications of this policy are clear: Apparently Congress regarded reservations as transitionary steps between "primitive" and "modern" society. As soon as a group achieved a margin of success (according to the ethnocentric standards of American culture), a reservation ceased to have a rationale for existence. This self-serving attitude totally ignores both the political circumstances which brought about the reservation system in the first place (e.g., aboriginal right of title), and the legal treaties and sanctions which supposedly protected it.

Two of the most economically self-sustaining tribes, the Klamath in Oregon and the Menominee in Wisconsin, were located in timberland areas and operated logging industries. The government exerted tremendous pressure, employing levers of doubtful legal and ethical practice, and the manipulation of misunderstanding, to force these tribes to submit to termination. Whether this consent was ever actually granted in either case is a debatable point, but it is clear that neither group, had it sufficiently understood the policy, would have agreed.

Termination meant the absolute cessation, in exchange for a monetary settlement, of any special treaty arrangements or status which existed between the tribe and its members and the United States government. Upon termination, the Menominees would be expected, in legal effect, to cease being Indians and to somehow turn themselves into Wisconsonians overnight. On a date set by the government, the dependent, sovereign Menominee Nation, hundreds of years old, would become simply another county within the state.

Historical retrospect clearly shows that in all cases the termination policy was even more ill-conceived and socially disruptive than the Allotment policy had been before it—and just as illegal. The net effects of termination were the loss of large amounts of valuable land by the tribes involved, plus an enormous psychological blow to thousands of Indian people. The fallacy of the policy was patently obvious so quickly that it was suspended shortly after implementation, sparing other tribes similar losses. To date, one of the victimized tribes, the Menominee, has, through persistent and valiant efforts of a group of its members, managed to be reestablished as a reservation in 1973. But as a direct result of termination, the new Menominee lands were much smaller and poorer than the reservation had been before 1953.

Subsequent government policies aimed at assimilating the Native American were more subtle. Among these were the urban relocation programs, often hastily conceived and poorly managed attempts to induce Native Americans to migrate to cities. A substantial percentage of the participants in these programs eventually returned, frustrated and cynical, to their reservations.

Since World War II, pan-Indian political and social associations, such as the National Congress of American Indians (1944), the National Indian Youth Council (1961), and the American Indian Movement (1968), have been organized. These organizations reflect the growing consciousness of a cross-tribal ethnic identity among many Native Americans and their felt need for united responses to commonly shared problems.

The occupation of Alcatraz by the Indians of all tribes in 1969, for instance, ushered in a new era of Native American activism.

While all organizations could agree that a major end result of their activities should be a recommitment by the United States government to honor existing legal treaties, they often differed in regard to the tactics employed to bring this about. NCAI has maintained an effective congressional lobby, NIYC has concentrated on legal redress, and AIM, through its occupation of the Bureau of Indian Affairs building in Washington and the village of Wounded Knee, South Dakota, as well as inner-city programs aimed at urban Indian people, has engaged in direct confrontation politics together with court tests of treaty applicability.

In the northernmost state, the Alaska Federation of Natives, composed of representatives from Indian, Aleut, and Eskimo communities, was formed to combat the increasing governmental and state demand for oil-rich land. After years of fighting in the courts, a Native Land Claims settlement was finally reached. The compromise result, composed of a recompense in both land and money, was based largely on the age-old principles of aboriginal right of title—the same legal argument which inspired the earliest Native American–European agreements of the seventeenth century.

Increasingly, conflicts have arisen over questions of sovereignty and control of reservation land. The federal government has delegated many of its treaty responsibilities toward Native communities to states—often with disastrous results. Disputes over federal guarantees of Indian hunting and fishing rights have occurred from Washington to Minnesota to New York. The position of some states has been that since they never made any agreement with a tribe, they are therefore not bound by that tribe's federal treaty.

In the field of education, there is a growing demand for Indian control of school boards in Native American communities, and also for the employment of Native American teachers to work in the schools. Throughout the country, a number of Indian junior colleges have been established, and "survival schools" in urban centers such as St. Paul and Milwaukee aim at preserving the ethnic identity of Native children in the city.

The problems of urban Native Americans—poverty, discrimination, poor education and health care, crime, and alcoholism—are among the most serious and complex of any issues facing Indian people today. Many Native American people are beginning to insist that greater federal protection and attention be given to those Indians who are still tribal members but reside in urban centers.

Three quarters into the twentieth century, almost five hundred years after the first confused contacts between Europe and America and two hundred years after United States independence, Native Americans still fight on a variety of fronts and in a multitude of ways for ethnic survival and the right to be themselves. It is time the misunderstanding ended and the myths about Native American people were buried once and for all.

There are many things Indian people are not: They are not and never have been a unified, homogenous population; they are not represented by the stereotypes of Hollywood or most fiction; they are not peoples without history, languages, literatures, sciences, and arts; they are not vanished, and they are not vanishing. White American unlearning about Native American people could be the most promising beginning to a real understanding between cultures. It could pave the way for the kind of cultural respect necessary to the belief that, after all, Indian people *do* know what is best for themselves. This realization could, in turn, insure a much more peaceful and harmonious Native American future.

Indian people have weathered every conceivable storm and are here to tell the tale. The traditions and cultures, the world views and views of self, rooted in Native American societies may well offer solutions to problems confronting people in every land. Native Americans today are very much a part of the modern world. Their future is now.

PREFACE TO THE PHOTOGRAPHS

The geographical areas in which the photographs in this book are clustered could be introduced in any number of ways. The position of Native Americans in modern America is paradoxical and often contradictory. Native people can be viewed with some validity as either prototypical victims of a European dream (some would call it a nightmare) of America or quintessential heroes, hanging on, battered and bleeding, but *winning* because they didn't lose. In a way both images are true, not just one or the other; tragedy and humor, suffering and strength, are multiple sides of a single coin—and not necessarily only a nickle.

Less meaningful and more unforgivable is the attempt to view Native Americans, past or present, through the rosy-colored, "Red Skin" producing glasses of stereotype. *The* Native American is not good or bad, noble or savage, ecological or drunken, though *some* individuals no doubt incorporate one, two, or all of these traits. For the best of intentions and with the worst results, make-believe Indians have stalked YMCA's and Boy Scout camps, TV commercials and college banners, and in the last analysis have only served to dehumanize and disguise the reality of those they pretend to represent. One might well conclude that the only good *dead* Indian would be Billy Jack!

The sections, then, are framed only in general terms and with an emphasis on the most positive and significant programs and developments in their respective areas. In most cases these photographs will tell their own story and will be interpreted differently according to their viewer. The introductory comments are intended to place them in a factual yet optimistic context and to take the long-term rather than the short-term historical view.

ALASKA

ALASKA

- Town or city with 250 or more Indians
- Federal Indian reservation
- Native regional corporations

200 KILOMETERS

200 MILES

ARCTIC OCEAN

CANADA

Barrow

Wainwright

Point Hope

Kotzebue
Noatak
Kiana
Noorvik
Selawik

DIOMEDE IS.
WALES

Nome

Savoonga

Gambell

Emanguk

Hooper Bay

Tununak

Chevak

Toksook Bay

Mountain Village
St. Marys
Pilot Station
Akolmiut
Bethel
Akiachak
Kwethluk
Napaiskak

Kipnuk
Kwinhagak

UNALAKLEET
Unalakleet

Nulato
Galena

Fort Yukon

VENETIE

Fairbanks

Anchorage
Spenard

CHUGACH

Gulf of Alaska

KLUKWAN

Juneau

Hoona

Angoon

Kake

Wrangell
ANNETTE I.
Ketchikan
Metlakatla

SEALASKA
Sitka
Mount Edgecumbe

Togiak
Dillingham

Kodiak
Old Harbor

KARLUK

KONIAG

St. Paul

AKUTAN
ALEUT

ALEUT

Bering Sea

INDEX MAP

Alaska is both a last stand and a new beginning for Native societies in America. Its history of Native-white contact is shorter, in some cases less intense and less bitter than in any other area of the United States. Alaskan Native societies, while retaining much of their traditional language, culture, and art, have banded together in the 1970's to form Native Corporations which are viable political and economic forces.

The Alaska Native Land Claims settlement promises a greater fiscal independence, and the subsurface wealth of much of the Native-controlled land bodes well for a developing future. In Alaska, where almost twenty percent of the permanent population is Indian, Eskimo, or Aleut, Native people sit in the state legislature and run, as candidates of major political parties, for national office.

The Alaska Federation of Natives, toughened in the long but successful fight it has waged for Native rights during the past decade, has the confidence and respect of Native people throughout the state and the country.

There is hope here. The human, cultural, and material resources of Alaska assure it a key role in the Native American tomorrow.

An Eskimo whaling camp off Point Barrow, the northernmost
place on the American continent. The dark part
of the sky is a reflection from the Arctic Sea and
helps travelers find their way.

Eskimo whalers use traditional principles but modern equipment. Motorized sleds replace dog teams and outboard motors drive their umiaks.

The large dangerous piles are due to breaking and freezing of the ice.

Starting out with modern gun, buoys, nylon rope, and harpoons.

Barrow, second largest Eskimo town in Alaska.

With no darkness in summer, children play at any hour.

Dogs are kept mostly for sport.

A traditional dance.

The audience.

Children of Barrow, invited to fly to Fairbanks by its business clubs, to attend a circus performance.

Pipe at Prudhoe Bay for the line to Valdez.

*The oil industry is employing thousands of workers;
unfortunately too few are native Alaskans.*

Denali,
the Indian name for Mt. McKinley.

Caribou still travel extensively.

Dahl sheep roam the mountainsides.

Trains and moose often collide in winter, killing many animals.

An Athapascan girl guides tourists on a Tanana River boat.

Drying fish at a village along the river.

The Greek Orthodox religion brought to America by the Russians is practiced today by many native Alaskans.

The priest also occasionally acts as storekeeper.

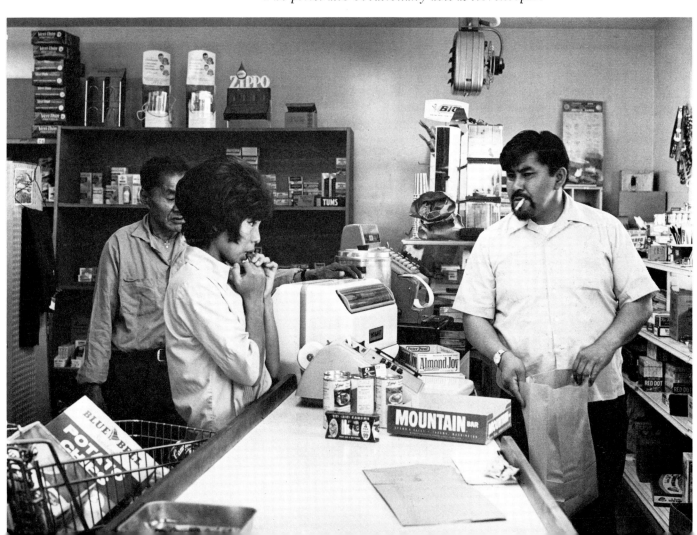

Icebergs break off from the large glaciers.

A delta is being formed.

Hoona depends on her fishing boats. Planes are used almost like buses where there are no roads.

Traditional decoration for modern industry.

Native languages were suppressed by the federal government.
Now they are being taught.

A class in Tlingit.

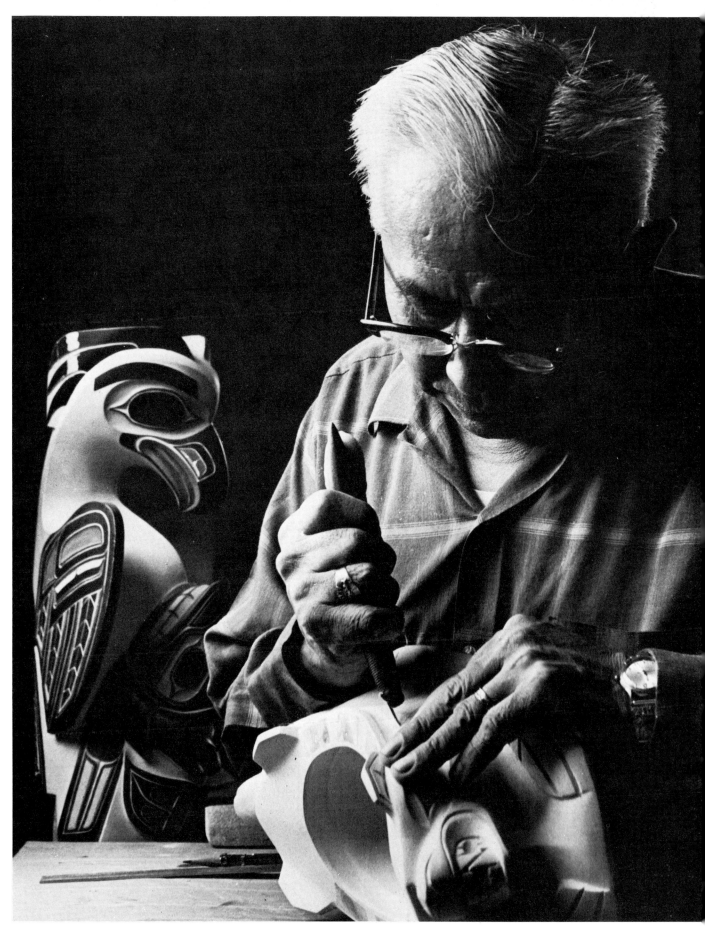

Carvers are highly respected in the land of totem poles.

A Haida captain.

Teaching the Haida story of the great flood.

Clams are a delicacy.

Hunting is useful and fun.

*Totem poles brought from original sites are waiting for a
museum. They told about family and community history.*

New totems are either copies of original ones or creations in the spirit of the old.

Totems can serve as either a record of family or cultural history or simply as nonfunctional art.

Traditional religious ceremonies were prohibited by the federal government until 1934. These costumes had been in hiding for many years.

Clear-cutting is ugly, and the washed soil kills hatching fish.

Lumber mills pollute the air and water.

THE FAR WEST

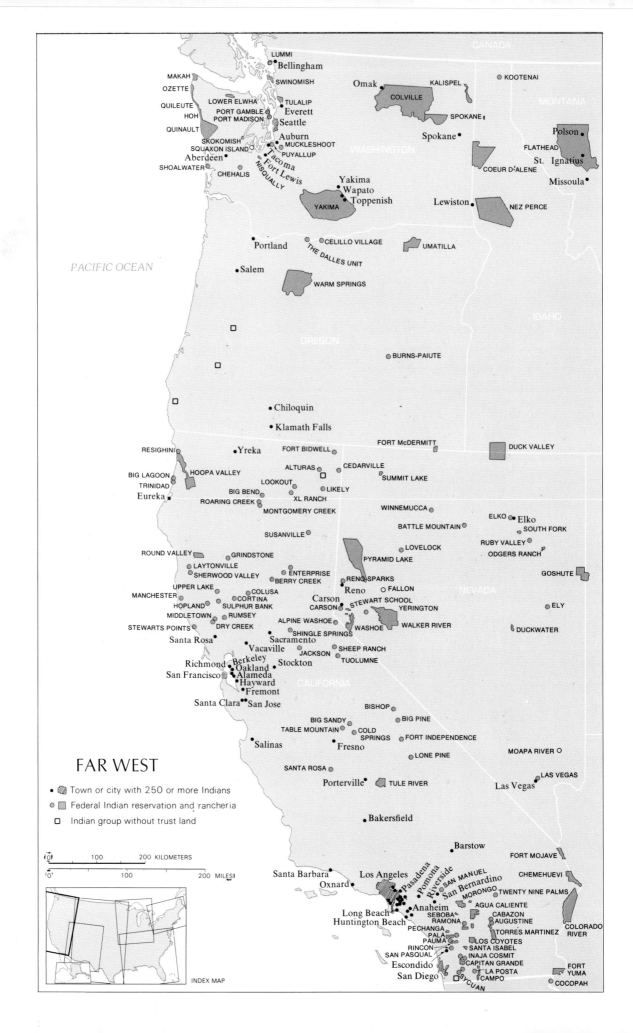

FAR WEST

- ● ▨ Town or city with 250 or more Indians
- ⊙ ▦ Federal Indian reservation and rancheria
- ▢ Indian group without trust land

100   200 KILOMETERS

100   200 MILES

INDEX MAP

PACIFIC OCEAN

CANADA

MONTANA

WASHINGTON

OREGON

IDAHO

NEVADA

CALIFORNIA

LUMMI
Bellingham
MAKAH
OZETTE
SWINOMISH
Omak
KALISPEL
COLVILLE
KOOTENAI
QUILEUTE
LOWER ELWHA
TULALIP
HOH
PORT GAMBLE
Everett
SPOKANE
QUINAULT
PORT MADISON
Seattle
SKOKOMISH
Auburn
Spokane
Polson
SQUAXON ISLAND
MUCKLESHOOT
FLATHEAD
Aberdeen
PUYALLUP
St. Ignatius
SHOALWATER
Tacoma
COEUR D'ALENE
CHEHALIS
Fort Lewis
Missoula
NISQUALLY
Yakima
Wapato
Lewiston
NEZ PERCE
YAKIMA
Toppenish
Portland
CELILLO VILLAGE
UMATILLA
THE DALLES UNIT
Salem
WARM SPRINGS
BURNS-PAIUTE
Chiloquin
Klamath Falls
FORT McDERMITT
RESIGHINI
Yreka
FORT BIDWELL
DUCK VALLEY
BIG LAGOON
HOOPA VALLEY
ALTURAS
CEDARVILLE
TRINIDAD
LOOKOUT
SUMMIT LAKE
Eureka
BIG BEND
LIKELY
ROARING CREEK
XL RANCH
WINNEMUCCA
MONTGOMERY CREEK
ELKO
Elko
BATTLE MOUNTAIN
SOUTH FORK
SUSANVILLE
RUBY VALLEY
LOVELOCK
ODGERS RANCH
ROUND VALLEY
GRINDSTONE
PYRAMID LAKE
GOSHUTE
LAYTONVILLE
SHERWOOD VALLEY
ENTERPRISE
RENO SPARKS
UPPER LAKE
BERRY CREEK
Reno
FALLON
ELY
MANCHESTER
COLUSA
Carson
STEWART SCHOOL
HOPLAND
CORTINA
CARSON
YERINGTON
MIDDLETOWN
SULPHUR BANK
DUCKWATER
RUMSEY
ALPINE WASHOE
STEWARTS POINTS
DRY CREEK
WASHOE
WALKER RIVER
SHINGLE SPRINGS
Santa Rosa
Sacramento
Vacaville
SHEEP RANCH
Berkeley
JACKSON
Richmond
Oakland
Stockton
TUOLUMNE
San Francisco
Alameda
Hayward
Fremont
Santa Clara
San Jose
BISHOP
BIG SANDY
BIG PINE
TABLE MOUNTAIN
COLD
Salinas
SPRINGS
FORT INDEPENDENCE
Fresno
LONE PINE
MOAPA RIVER
SANTA ROSA
Porterville
TULE RIVER
LAS VEGAS
Bakersfield
Las Vegas
Barstow
FORT MOJAVE
Santa Barbara
Los Angeles
Pasadena
CHEMEHUEVI
Oxnard
Pomona
SAN MANUEL
Riverside
San Bernardino
TWENTY NINE PALMS
MORONGO
AGUA CALIENTE
Long Beach
Anaheim
CABAZON
Huntington Beach
SEBOBA
RAMONA
AUGUSTINE
COLORADO
PECHANGA
TORRES MARTINEZ
RIVER
PALA
PAUMA
LOS COYOTES
RINCON
SANTA ISABEL
SAN PASQUAL
INAJA COSMIT
Escondido
CAPITAN GRANDE
FORT
LA POSTA
YUMA
San Diego
CAMPO
SYCUAN
COCOPAH

In traditional times, the Far West area was the most densely populated and at the same time the most culturally diversified region of North America. In many respects it remains so today.

Contemporary California has been the center of much that is significant in national Native American affairs. The occupation of Alcatraz on November 14, 1969, initiated a new era in Native American activism, and the California Indian Education Association has spearheaded the national movement for curricular reform of materials dealing with Indian history. Scholarly journals, such as *The Indian Historian*, and popular Native periodicals are published in the Bay Area and distributed throughout the country.

To the north, the state of Washington was the site for one of the first major tests of Public Law 280, and the ensuing fishing rights controversy has established important legal precedents for Native Americans in all parts of the United States.

In Oregon, the Klamath Nation, unilaterally abolished by the government as a reservation in 1961 under the disastrous termination policy, has announced its intent to win reinstitution.

The Native populations of Los Angeles, Seattle, Tacoma, Portland, Oakland, and San Francisco are large and growing larger. And the Far West remains, as it always has been, a microcosm of the enormous heterogeneity and dynamism of Native American societies.

The Lummi Stomish, a water festival, brings visitors and competitors from long distances.

International canoe races are a feature of the event.

Preparing a salmon feast.

Indoor activities include dancing and electing a queen.

Fishing rights were agreed upon with the federal government before there was a state of Washington.

*There have been bloody struggles between Indians and
officers enforcing state laws, later ruled by the Supreme Court
to be in violation of treaty rights.*

The Quinault River outlet.

Net fishing, practiced freely because the river is on reservation land.

Outside the Indian center for the San Francisco Bay Area.

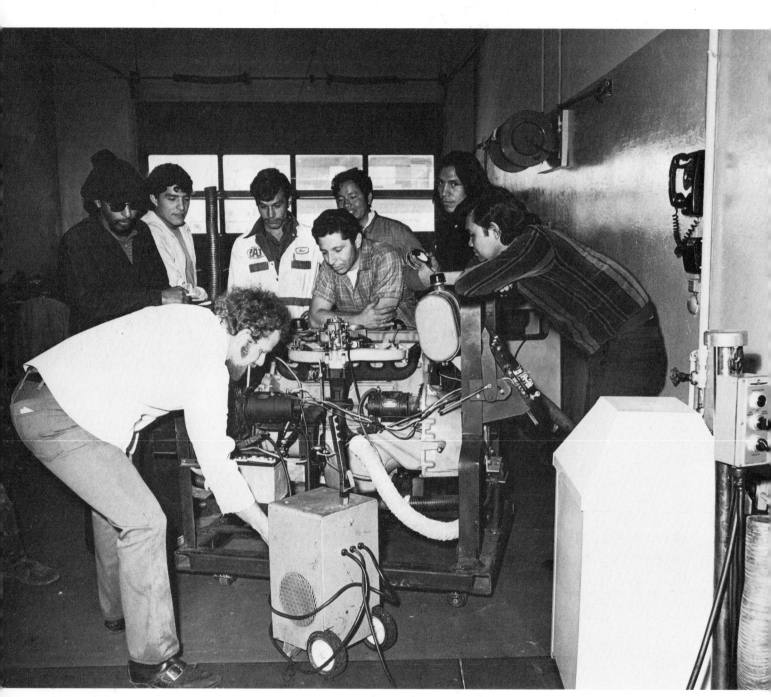

Training auto mechanics.

Inside the Indian center.

An alcoholics' rehabilitation center.

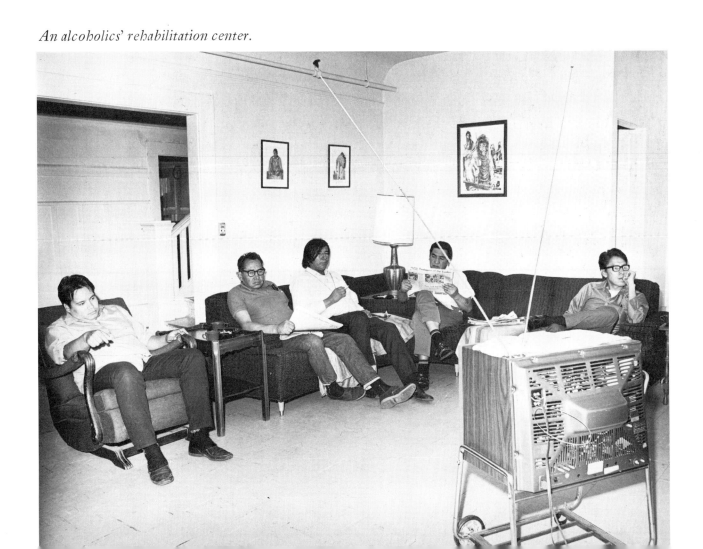

Alcatraz might have been a symbol of "Peace on Earth."

Irrigation for the Cocopas.

Home.

An old Cocopa.

A member of the Tribal Council.

A Quechan woman in Yuma.

Lovers of Yuma, they said.

The last territorial jail.

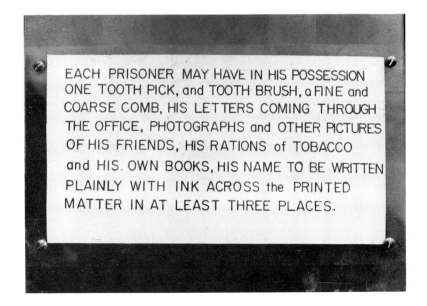

EACH PRISONER MAY HAVE IN HIS POSSESSION ONE TOOTH PICK, and TOOTH BRUSH, a FINE and COARSE COMB, HIS LETTERS COMING THROUGH THE OFFICE, PHOTOGRAPHS and OTHER PICTURES OF HIS FRIENDS, HIS RATIONS of TOBACCO and HIS. OWN BOOKS, HIS NAME TO BE WRITTEN PLAINLY WITH INK ACROSS the PRINTED MATTER IN AT LEAST THREE PLACES.

Head Start in Yuma.

A premed student.

In native Laguna dress.

THE SOUTHWEST

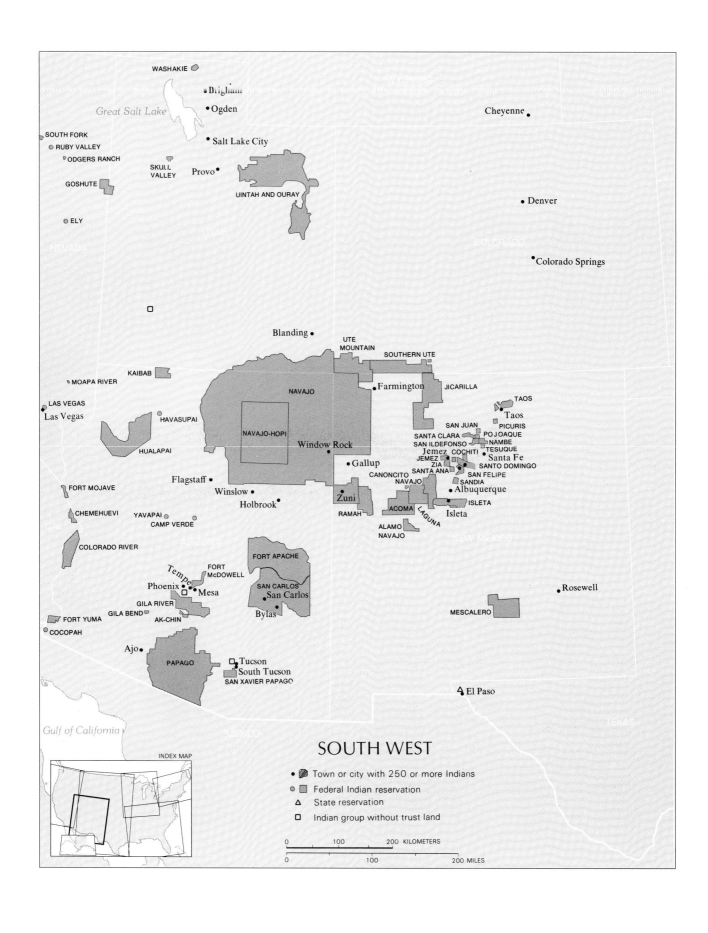

WASHAKIE

•Brigham

Great Salt Lake

•Ogden

Cheyenne•

SOUTH FORK
○ RUBY VALLEY
▽ ODGERS RANCH

•Salt Lake City

SKULL
VALLEY   Provo•

GOSHUTE

UINTAH AND OURAY

Denver•

○ ELY

NEVADA

UTAH

COLORADO

Colorado Springs•

KAIBAB

Blanding •

UTE
MOUNTAIN

SOUTHERN UTE

TAOS

MOAPA RIVER

LAS VEGAS
Las Vegas•

HAVASUPAI

NAVAJO

Farmington•

JICARILLA

Taos

SAN JUAN

PICURIS

POJOAQUE

SANTA CLARA
SAN ILDEFONSO

NAMBE

NAVAJO-HOPI

Window Rock•

JEMEZ   COCHITI   TESUQUE
Jemez

TAOS•

Santa Fe

HUALAPAI

•Gallup

JEMEZ
ZIA

SANTO DOMINGO

SAN FELIPE

FORT MOJAVE

Flagstaff•

CANONCITO
NAVAJO

SANTA ANA

SANDIA

Winslow•

•Albuquerque

CHEMEHUEVI

YAVAPAI   ○
CAMP VERDE

Holbrook•

Zuni•

ACOMA   LAGUNA

ISLETA
Isleta

COLORADO RIVER

ARIZONA

RAMAH

ALAMO
NAVAJO

NEW MEXICO

FORT APACHE

Rosewell•

Tempe
FORT
McDOWELL

Phoenix□ •Mesa

SAN CARLOS

FORT YUMA

GILA RIVER

San Carlos

MESCALERO

COCOPAH

GILA BEND
AK-CHIN

Bylas•

Ajo•

PAPAGO

□•Tucson
South Tucson

SAN XAVIER PAPAGO

⊿El Paso

Gulf of California

MEXICO

TEXAS

SOUTH WEST

• Town or city with 250 or more Indians

○ □ Federal Indian reservation

△   State reservation

□   Indian group without trust land

INDEX MAP

0   100   200 KILOMETERS

0   100   200 MILES

The Southwest is a land of great contrasts. Within it many Native American people continue to live almost exclusively by the traditions of their ancestors. They speak their own languages and keep active the ancient wisdom, literature, and science of their tribes.

Also in the Southwest are found other Native Americans, no less Indian, who work in both the tribal and national arenas in an attempt to improve the economic, educational, and legal status of their people. These men and women are often fluently bilingual and can move with practiced skill between their own and American culture.

The Navajo Nation, located in the heart of the Southwest, is the country's largest tribe in both population and area. As such it is highly influential, and experimental programs conducted there have a national Native American impact. It is here that some of the greatest innovations in Indian education have been created, such as the intensive development of Navajo language curricula, the all-Navajo Rough Rock Demonstration School, and the fully accredited Navajo Community College.

Other southwestern tribes have also begun to assume a national and even international leadership role. Representatives of the Hopi people, for instance, were sent to counsel a worldwide assembly of scientists in Stockholm gathered to discuss problems of the environment.

In the Southwest, perhaps more than in any other area, the traditions of leadership, strength, and wisdom of the Native American past blend with those of the present. The directions and activities charted here will necessarily affect the opportunities of Indian people throughout the land.

Sunset in Monument Valley.

San Carlos Apaches.

Mulchatha, Pima reservation.

Rodeos are greatly enjoyed in the West by Indian participants and observers.

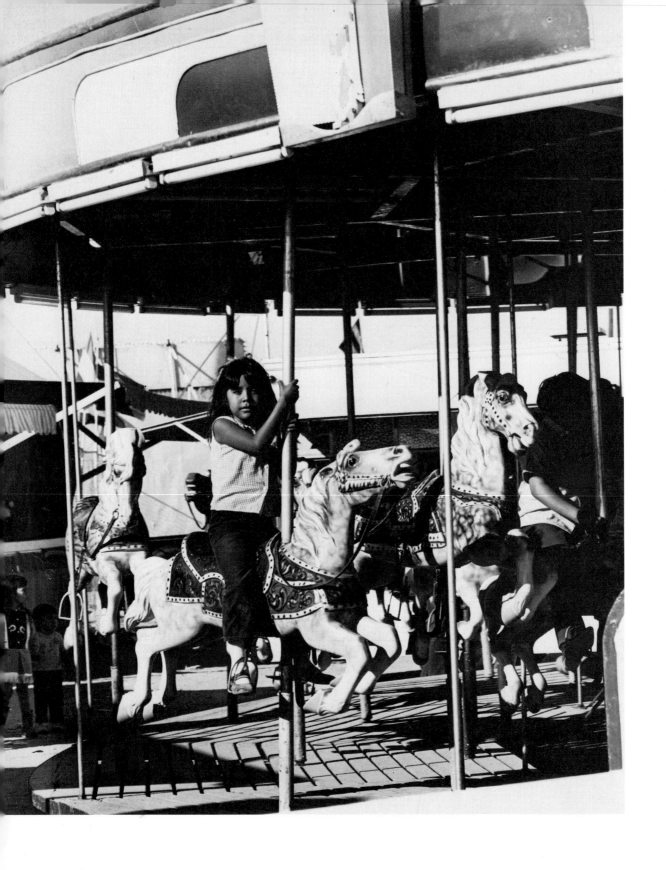

A ceremonial dance.

The Canyon de Chelly, inhabited for thousands of years.

Cliff dwellers wanted safety from enemies.

Making bread.

Weaving in a summer house.

Corn has been grown here for centuries.

Encampment for Flagstaff "Powwow," organized by the chamber of commerce but attended by thousands of Indians.

Renewing old friendship.

An amusement area.

Teen-Agers.

The Navajo capital, Window Rock.

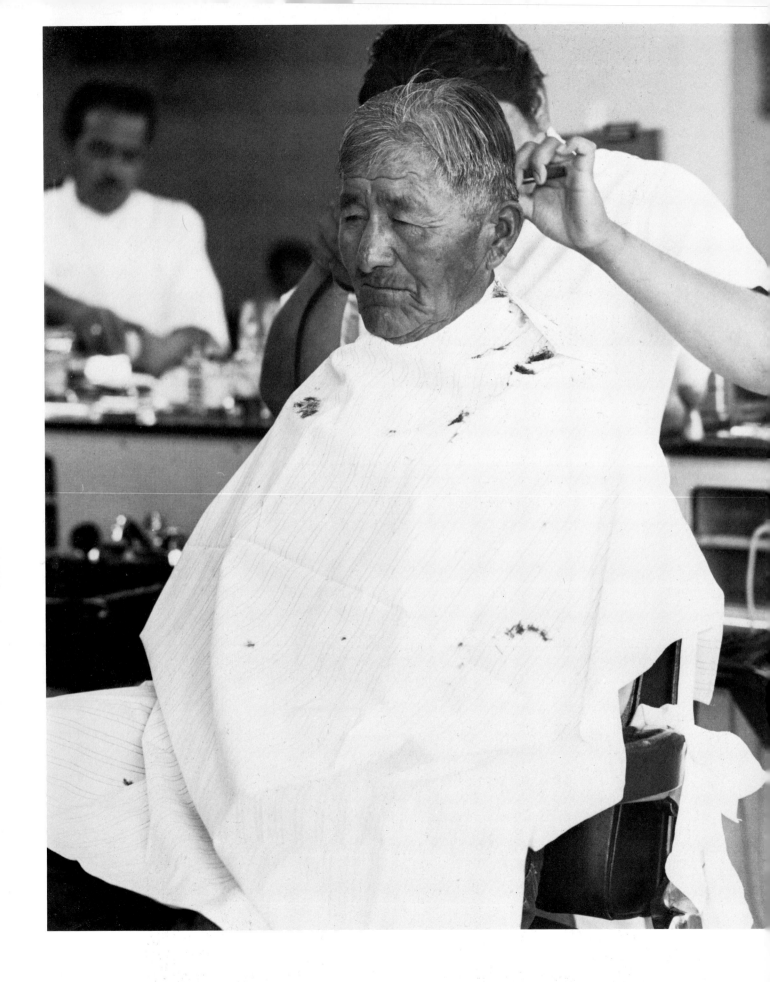

A silversmith.

An electronics plant.

A Navajo lumbermill.

Navajo forest.

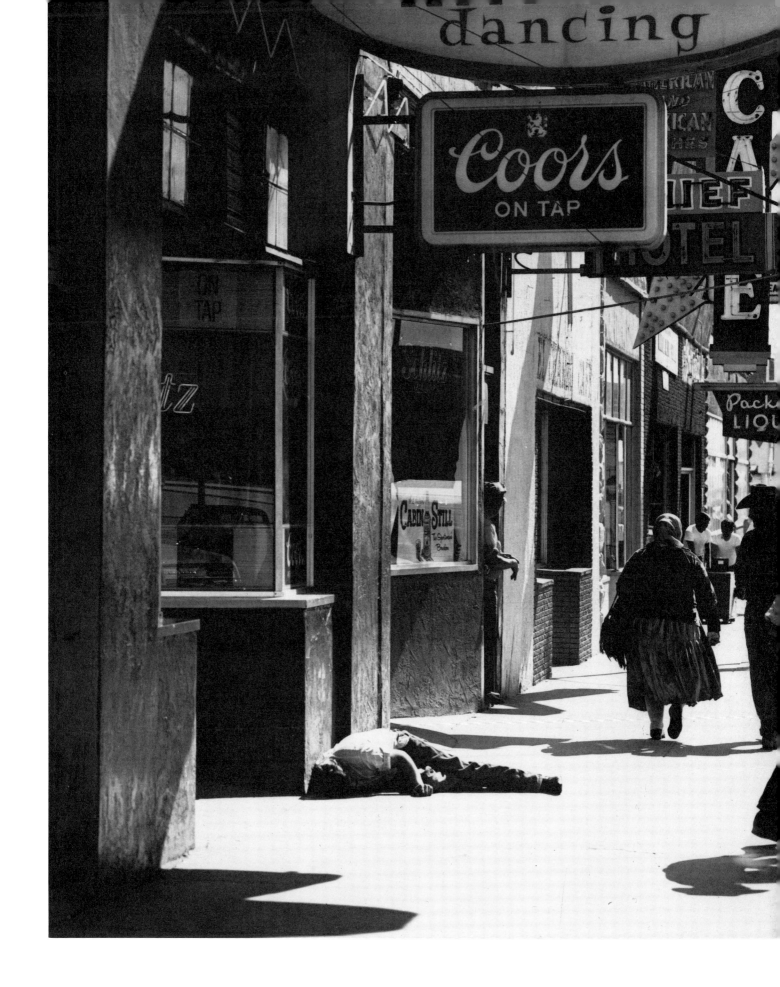

Controversial strip mining.

Arches in Monument Valley.

A hogan.

A summer hogan.

Herding sheep, a major occupation.

A trading post.

A hospital.

The valley of the Rio Grande.

Acoma.

Sacred mesa.

Evening in Taos.

Fresh bread.

Farms outside Taos.

New construction in Taos.

Bread ovens in San Ildefonso.

Horses in Taos.

Puye festival.

Mr. Chairman, the pride of the Picuris pueblo and the pride of all people who know him.

Tesuque baseball.

A Picuris kiva (ceremonial building).

A kachina doll.

Fritz Scholder.

R. C. Gorman.

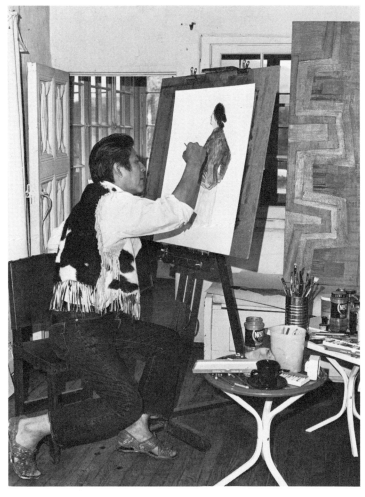

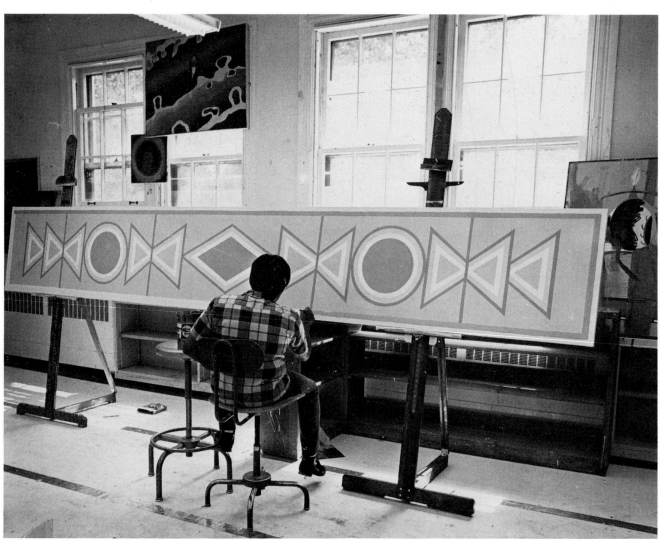

Santa Fe Indian Art Institute.

Enlarging a prize-winning model.

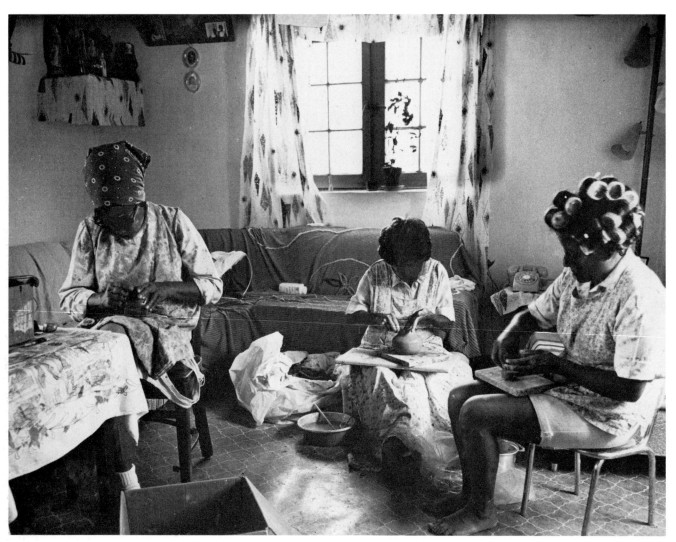

Family potters.

Rosa Gonzalez.

THE PLAINS

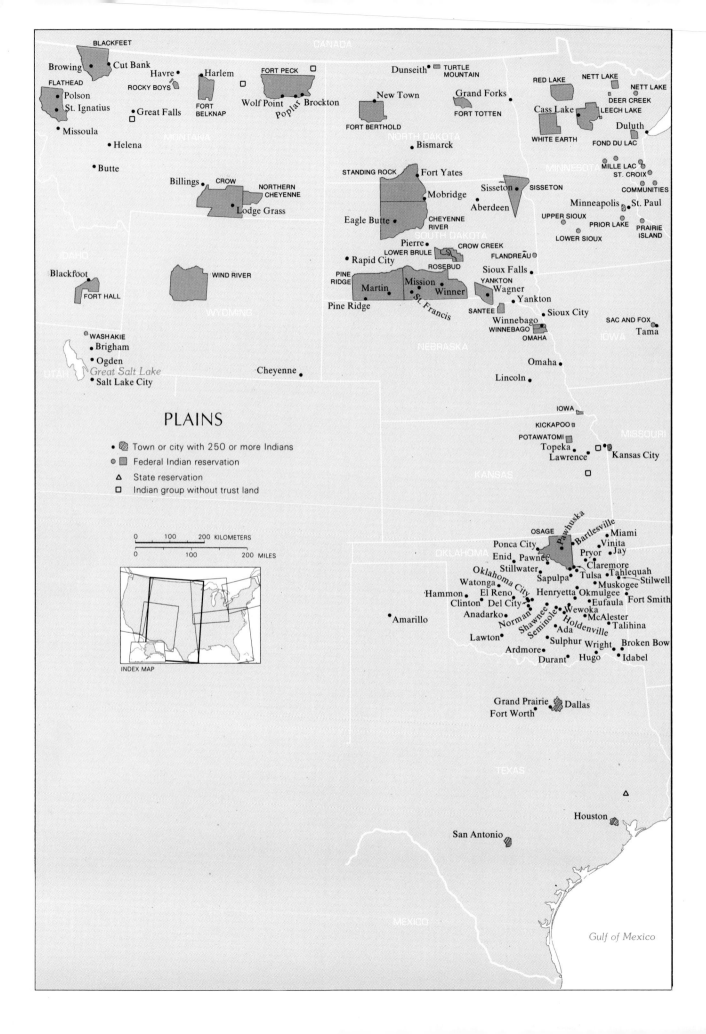

PLAINS

- 🏙 Town or city with 250 or more Indians
- ◉ ▨ Federal Indian reservation
- △ State reservation
- ▢ Indian group without trust land

0   100   200 KILOMETERS

0   100   200 MILES

INDEX MAP

CANADA

BLACKFEET
Browing   Cut Bank
FLATHEAD   Havre
    Harlem   FORT PECK
Polson   ROCKY BOYS
St. Ignatius   FORT   Wolf Point   Brockton
    BELKNAP   Poplar
Great Falls
Missoula

MONTANA

Helena

Butte

Billings   CROW   NORTHERN
    CHEYENNE
    Lodge Grass

IDAHO

Blackfoot   WIND RIVER
FORT HALL

WYOMING

WASHAKIE
Brigham
Ogden
Great Salt Lake
UTAH   Salt Lake City

Cheyenne

Dunseith   TURTLE
    MOUNTAIN

New Town   Grand Forks

FORT BERTHOLD   FORT TOTTEN

NORTH DAKOTA
Bismarck

STANDING ROCK   Fort Yates

Mobridge   Sisseton   SISSETON

Eagle Butte   CHEYENNE   Aberdeen
    RIVER

Pierre   SOUTH DAKOTA
    LOWER BRULE   CROW CREEK
Rapid City   FLANDREAU
    ROSEBUD   Sioux Falls
PINE   YANKTON
RIDGE   Mission   Wagner
Martin   Winner
Pine Ridge   St. Francis   Yankton
    SANTEE
    Winnebago   Sioux City
    WINNEBAGO
    OMAHA

NEBRASKA

Omaha

Lincoln

IOWA

KICKAPOO

POTAWATOMI
Topeka
Lawrence

KANSAS

RED LAKE   NETT LAKE
    NETT LAKE
    DEER CREEK
Cass Lake   LEECH LAKE
    Duluth
WHITE EARTH   FOND DU LAC

MINNESOTA   MILLE LAC
    ST. CROIX

    COMMUNITIES
Minneapolis   St. Paul
UPPER SIOUX
    PRIOR LAKE   PRAIRIE
    ISLAND
LOWER SIOUX

SAC AND FOX
    Tama

IOWA

MISSOURI

Kansas City

OSAGE   Pawhuska   Bartlesville   Miami
Ponca City   Vinita   Jay
    Pryor
Enid   Pawnee   Claremore
    Stillwater   Sapulpa   Tulsa   Tahlequah
Oklahoma City   Muskogee   Stilwell
Watonga   Henryetta   Okmulgee   Fort Smith
Hammon   El Reno   Eufaula
Clinton   Del City   Wewoka
    Norman   McAlester
Anadarko   Shawnee   Holdenville   Talihina
    Seminole   Ada
Lawton   Sulphur   Wright   Broken Bow
    Ardmore   Durant   Hugo   Idabel

OKLAHOMA

Amarillo

Grand Prairie   Dallas
Fort Worth

TEXAS

Houston

San Antonio

MEXICO   Gulf of Mexico

In contrast to the monolithic Hollywood image of the Plains held by many non–Native Americans, this area remains one of the most culturally heterogeneous on the continent. This is due in part to the manner in which the area was populated. Certainly tribes inhabited the Plains in ancient times, but many more migrated from both east and west in the seventeenth and eighteenth centuries when the Spanish-imported horse made transportation and hunting within the area's enormous distances more possible. In the nineteenth century, a less voluntary but equally pluralistic wave of Indian people arrived, removed from their own lands throughout the United States by federal dictates.

Today, therefore, Plains culture is a combination of many traditions. The art, dance, and music produced here are dynamic and highly influential. The Native American Church was organized in the southern Plains and quickly found acceptance in other areas. The summer pow-wows of Plains tribes are meeting grounds and cultural events for Native American people throughout the country.

In recent years the Plains has emerged as an area in which nationally important Indian issues are decided. Huge deposits of coal in the West and oil in the South provide Native Americans the challenge of ecological, sane land management. The occupation of Wounded Knee and the ensuing legal struggles associated with it test the age-old questions of sovereignty and treaty viability.

The multicultural history of the Plains has evolved into a modern, pluralistic Native American society.

On the Plains.

A Kiowa contest.

A Kiowa-Apache-Comanche dance.

A Kiowa store.

A western Cherokee registers to vote.

Prefab homes.

The Housing Board.

Cherokee high school.

Electronics workers.

A Rosebud Sioux musician.

Buffalos roam but in protected areas.

Curing buffalo hides.

A recreation center.

Legal advice.

The range.

Separating cattle.

Branding.

Unloading for ranch feeding.

Graduation prom.

The funeral of Gabriel Lawrence Two Eagle, killed in
Vietnam, a brave Sioux who deserves to be honored by all
Americans.

THE BATTLE OF WOUNDED KNEE

(CONTINUED)

9:00 a.m. by a line of foot soldiers and cavalry. Chief Big Foot, sick with pneumonia, lay in a warmed tent provided by Col. Forsythe, in the center of the camp. A white flag flew there, placed by the Indians. Directly in the rear of the Indian Camp was a dry draw, running east and west.

The Indians were ordered to surrender their arms before proceeding to Pine Ridge. Capt. Wallace, with an Army detail, began searching the teepees for hidden weapons. During this excitement, Yellow Bird, a medicineman, walked among the braves, blowing on an eaglebone whistle, inciting the warriors to action, declaring that the "Ghost Shirts" worn by the warriors would protect them from the soldier's bullets. A shot was fired, and all hell broke loose. The troops fired a deadly volley into the Council warriors, killing nearly half of them. A bloody hand—to—hand struggle followed, all the more desperate since the Indians were armed mostly with clubs, knives, and revolvers. The Hotchkiss guns fired 2—pound explosive shells on the groups, indiscrim- inately killing warriors, women, children, and their own disarming soldiers. Soldiers were killed by cross—fire of their comrades in this desperate engagement.

Surviving Indians stampeded in wild disorder for the shelter of the draw 200 feet to the south, escaping west and east up the draw, and north down Wounded Knee Creek. Persuit by the 7th Cavalry resulted in the killing of more men, women and children, causing this battle to be referred to as the "Wounded Knee Massacre". One hour later, 146 indian , women and children lay dead in Wounded Knee Creek valley. The bodies of many were scattered along a distance two miles from the scene of the encounter. Twenty soldiers were killed on the field, and sixteen later died of wounds. Wounded soldiers and Indians alike were taken to Pine Ridge Agency. A blizzard came up. Four days later, an Army de- tail gathered up the Indian dead and buried them in a common grave at the top of the hill northwest of here. A mon- ument marks this grave.

"Ghost Dancing" ended with this encounter. The Wounded Knee battlefield is the site of the last armed conflict be- tween the Sioux Indians and the United States Army.

Oglala.

St. Marys Lake, part park, part reservation.

Main Street.

Blackfeet justice.

A playground.

A grandmother.

A cleanup squad.

Grazing.

A ranch barn.

Sunday ranching.

To a roundup.

Farmland rotation.

All-Indian Rodeo.

Canadian Blackfeet.

A northern Cheyenne playhouse.

THE LAKES

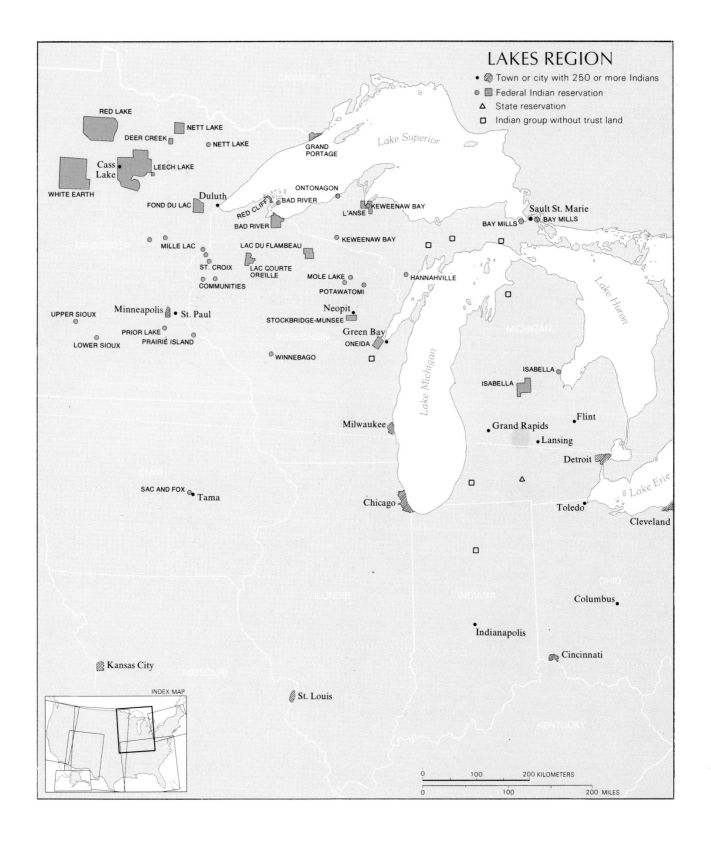

LAKES REGION

- ● ▨ Town or city with 250 or more Indians
- ● ■ Federal Indian reservation
- △ State reservation
- □ Indian group without trust land

CANADA

Lake Superior

RED LAKE

NETT LAKE

DEER CREEK

NETT LAKE

GRAND PORTAGE

Cass Lake

LEECH LAKE

WHITE EARTH

FOND DU LAC

Duluth

ONTONAGON

RED CLIFF BAD RIVER

BAD RIVER

L'ANSE KEWEENAW BAY

Sault St. Marie

BAY MILLS BAY MILLS

MILLE LAC

KEWEENAW BAY

MINNESOTA

ST. CROIX

LAC DU FLAMBEAU

LAC COURTE OREILLE

COMMUNITIES

MOLE LAKE

HANNAHVILLE

POTAWATOMI

MICHIGAN

Lake Huron

UPPER SIOUX

Minneapolis ● St. Paul

Neopit

STOCKBRIDGE-MUNSEE

PRIOR LAKE

LOWER SIOUX

PRAIRIE ISLAND

Green Bay

ONEIDA

WISCONSIN

WINNEBAGO

ISABELLA

ISABELLA

Lake Michigan

Flint

Grand Rapids

Lansing

Milwaukee

Detroit

IOWA

SAC AND FOX

Tama

Chicago

Toledo

Lake Erie

Cleveland

ILLINOIS

INDIANA

OHIO

Columbus

Indianapolis

Cincinnati

Kansas City

MISSOURI

INDEX MAP

St. Louis

KENTUCKY

0   100   200 KILOMETERS

0   100   200 MILES

The Midwestern territory bordering on Lakes Superior, Michigan, and Huron has, in recent years, become almost a microcosm of Native American life. Found here are large reservations where the traditional language, culture, economy and religion of individual tribes are strong and developing.

The Lakes region also contains, however, large Native American urban populations in cities like Minneapolis, St. Paul, Chicago, Duluth, and Milwaukee. In these communities, activities such as the AIM breakfast programs, Indian survival schools, and multidimensional cultural centers provide a means by which Native people far away from home can maintain their ethnic identity.

The Midwest is headquarters for the National Indian Education Association, a leader in the field of textbook reform and educational philosophy, and is the location of the first major Native American Studies Department in the country, established at the University of Minnesota.

Legal tests of Indian rights, from personal antidiscrimination cases to major judicial examinations of key treaties, have occurred in the Lakes region since 1960. The decisions reached here have implications for the future of Native American people in all parts of the United States.

Harvesting wild rice follows tradition—with the help of modern aluminum canoes.

Packing a day's work.

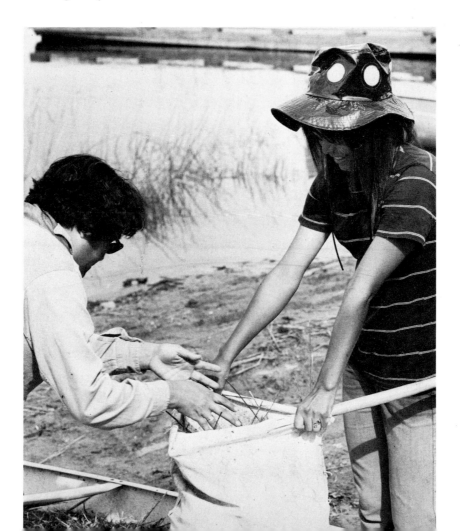

Overjoyed.

Weighing rice for sale.

Old-style parching.

An interfaith meeting.

A Chippewa U.S. marine recently discharged and falsely arrested, later exonerated.

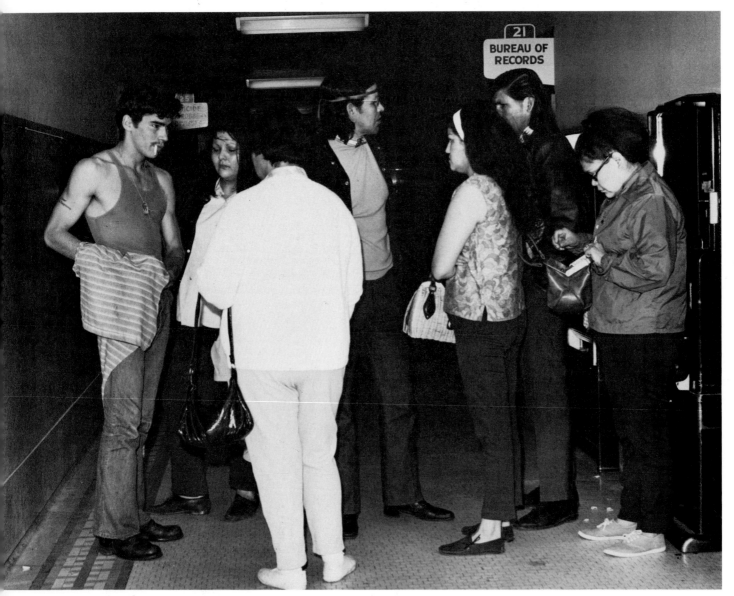

A clean shirt.

Preparing the defense.

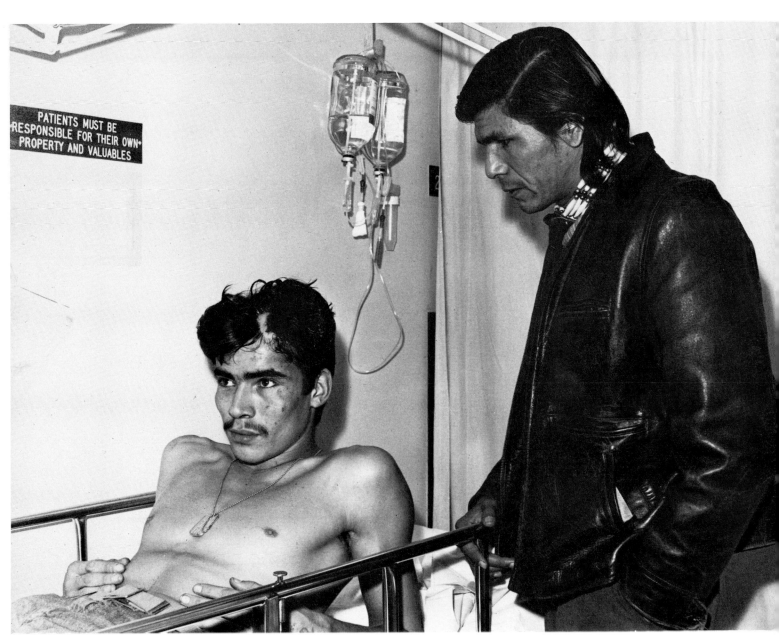

First aid.

THE NORTHEAST

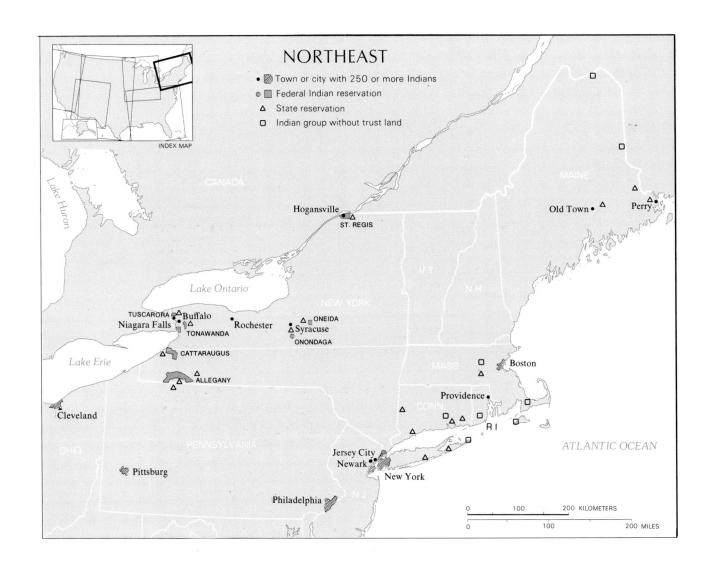

NORTHEAST

- ● ▨ Town or city with 250 or more Indians
- ● ▨ Federal Indian reservation
- △ State reservation
- ▢ Indian group without trust land

INDEX MAP

CANADA

Lake Huron

Lake Ontario

Lake Erie

Hogansville
ST. REGIS

MAINE

Old Town ● △   Perry △

VT

N.H

NEW YORK

TUSCARORA △ Buffalo
Niagara Falls   △
        TONAWANDA
● Rochester

△ ONEIDA
△ Syracuse
ONONDAGA

MASS   ▢   ▨ Boston
        △

△ CATTARAUGUS

Providence ●

△ ALLEGANY

CONN   ▢ △ ▢
        R I   ▢

▨ Cleveland

OHIO

PENNSYLVANIA

△

△

▢

△

ATLANTIC OCEAN

▨ Pittsburg

Jersey City ●
Newark ●▨
        New York

NJ

Philadelphia ▨

0   100   200 KILOMETERS

0   100   200 MILES

No group of Indian people in America has been under such constant and concerted pressure to disappear or assimilate as those of the Northeast. For four hundred years they have been evicted, missionized, and then ignored. Many of the treaty agreements governing relations between eastern tribes either predated the birth of the United States or were concluded with individual states rather than the federal government.

Today those Native Americans who survived in the East are re-emerging as a potent political and intellectual force. Federal recognition has been accorded, after complex judicial struggle, to an increasing number of tribes, and the recently formed Coalition of Eastern Native Americans promises to grow in influence and power. New industries based on centuries-old traditions are developing, from the manufacture of basketry and lacrosse sticks on some Iroquoian and Passamaquoddy reservations to the initiation of intensive aquaculture projects among the Shinnecocks of Long Island.

Organizations such as the Boston Indian Council and the American Indian Community House of New York assist urban Native Americans in maintaining contact with each other.

The tenacity and perseverance of the Native American people of the East in preserving strong cultural identities despite great odds is an inspiration to Indian people throughout the land.

High-steel construction attracts Indians. Many are Mohawks.

Unloading steel.

A Brooklyn Christmas party.

Native American Theatre Ensemble, rehearsal.

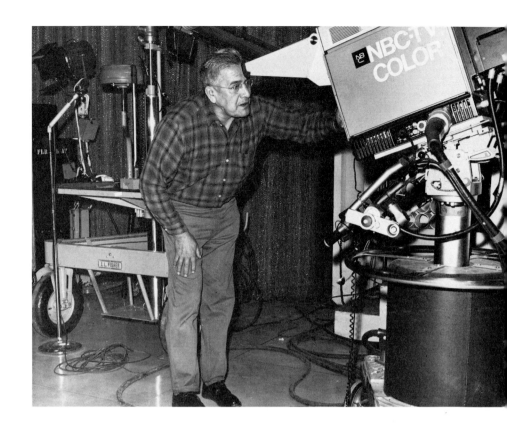

Final touches before performance.

Iroquois students on their way home from school.

Making lacrosse sticks.

THE SOUTHEAST

SOUTHEAST

- • ⬤ Town or city with 250 or more Indians
- ⊙ ▢ Federal Indian reservation
- △ State reservation
- ▢ Indian group without trust land

INDEX MAP

| 0 | 100 | 200 KILOMETERS |
| 0 | 100 | 200 MILES |

Kansas City

St. Louis

MISSOURI

Fort Smith

ARKANSAS

Memphis

ILLINOIS

INDIANA

Indianapolis

Cincinnati

OHIO

Columbus

KENTUCKY

TENNESSEE

Nashville-Davidson

CHEROKEE

Charlotte

MISSISSIPPI

ALABAMA

GEORGIA

CHOCTAW

LOUISIANA

CHITIMACHA

Houma

New Orleans

Gulf of Mexico

Atlanta

Jacksonville

FLORIDA

Tampa

BRIGHTON

Lake
Okeechobee

BIG CYPRESS

HOLLYWOOD
Hollywood
Miami

WEST VIRGINIA

Washington
Arlington

Baltimore

Richmond

VIRGINIA

Norfolk

High Point Greensboro

NORTH CAROLINA

Fort Bragg
Fayetteville
Pembroke Lumberton

SOUTH CAROLINA

ATLANTIC OCEAN

In 1820 Congress passed the Indian Removal Act, aimed at relocating all eastern Native American people to reservations west of the Mississippi. While many tribes had no choice but to submit, others managed to remain in or near their homelands. In the South, some Cherokees, Seminoles, and Choctaws virtually went into hiding for decades to avoid exile, and Lumbees were permitted to stay only because members of the Raleigh colony could be numbered among their ancestors.

In recent years, federal status and recognition have returned at last to tribes large and small throughout the Southeast. Major court decisions have favorably affected the position of the Lumbees, the Seminoles, and the Miccosukees, and organizations such as the United Southeastern Tribes have been formed to deal with Native American issues throughout the region.

Historically, important and far-reaching government policies toward Native Americans have originated in the South—for example, the nineteenth-century Supreme Court ruling defining a reservation as a sovereign, dependent nation. In the future the tribes of the area may be instrumental in convincing the American government to at last keep its promises.

On the Cherokee reservation.

A supermarket.

Loading prize bulls.

Ranching is profitable for the Seminoles.

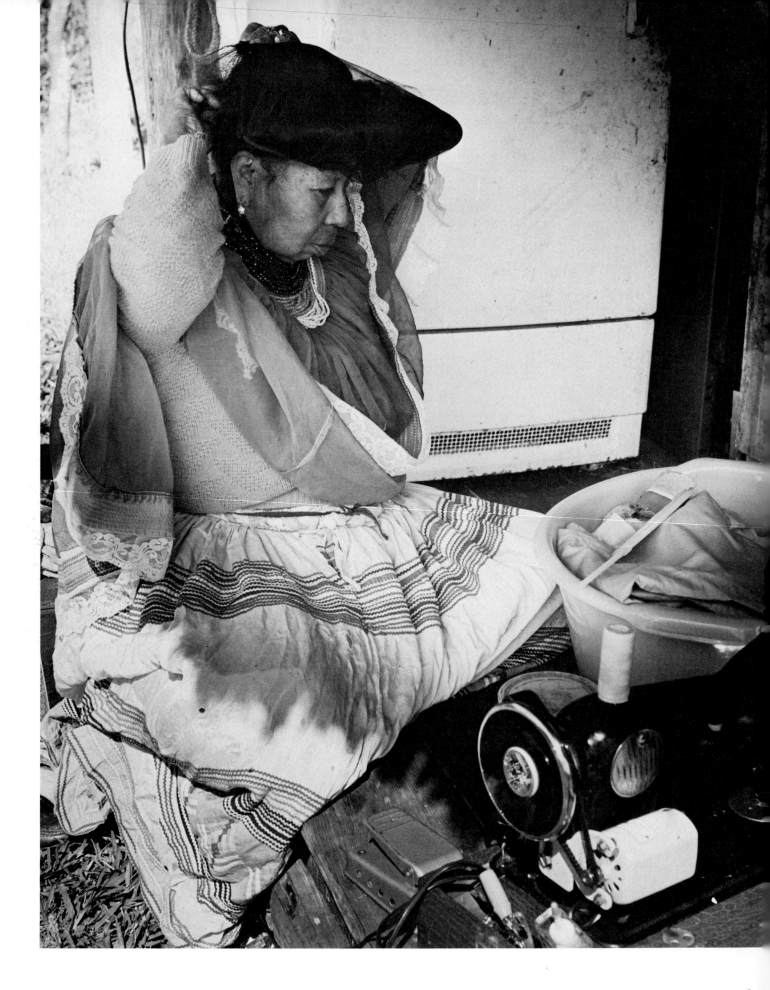

A Seminole matriarch.

The best mechanic in the area.

Road marker to Big Cypress.

Head Start.

A crowded home.

Tanning deerhide.

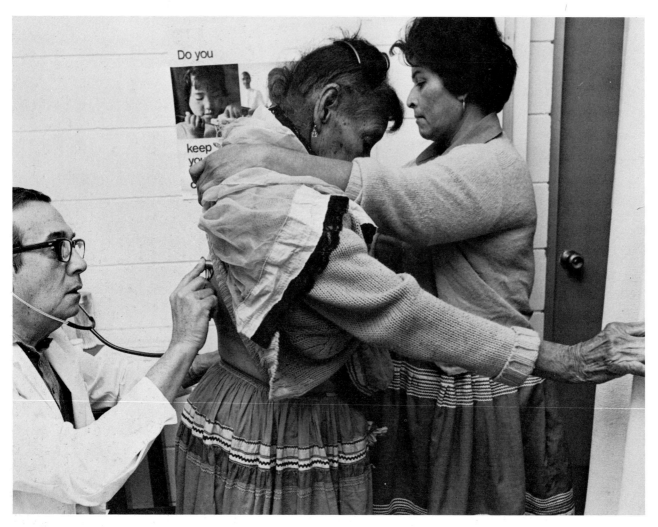

A clinic.

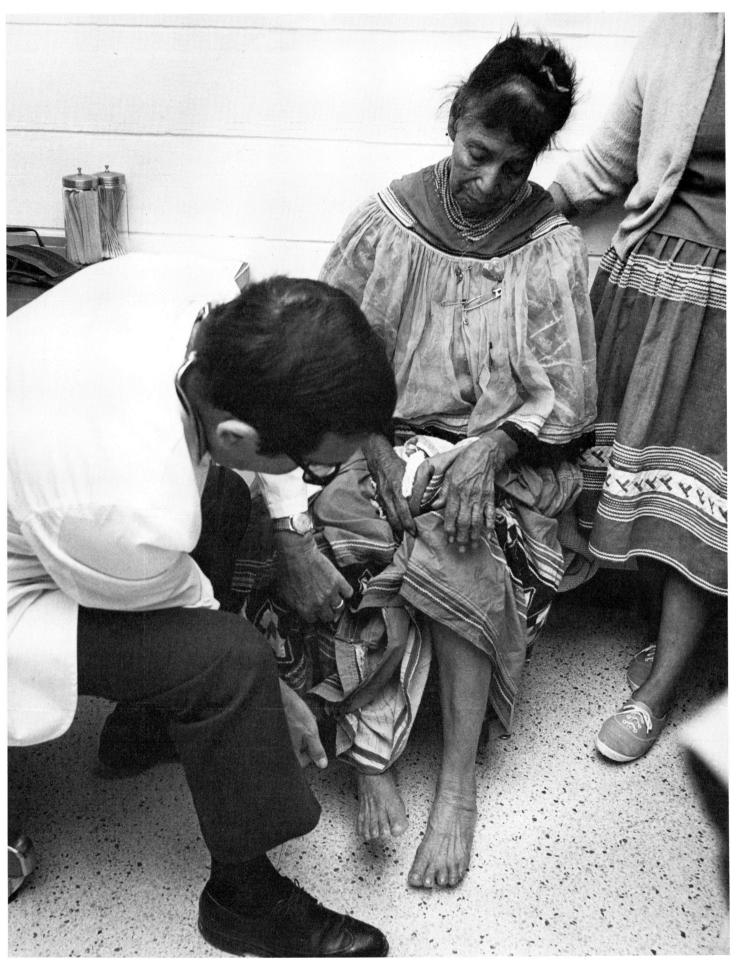

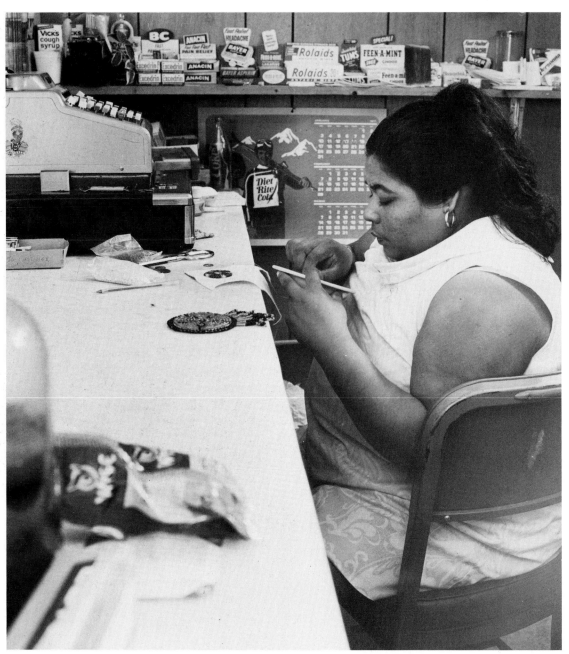

A Seminole reservation store.

A medicine man.

A dugout canoe being made.

A Miccosukee piloting an airboat to an Everglades camp.

The camp dock.

The typical fire is kept going by moving each log as it is consumed.

Miccosukee school.

SELECTED ADDITIONAL READINGS

AKWESASNE NOTES. *Voices From Wounded Knee, 1973.* Rooseveltown, N.Y.: 1974.

BAHR, H. M.; CHADWICK, B.; AND DAY, R. *Native Americans Today.* New York: Harper & Row, 1972.

BRANDON, WILLIAM (ed.). *The Magic World—American Indian Songs and Poems.* New York: William Morrow, 1971.

BURNETTE, ROBERT. *The Tortured Americans.* Englewood Cliffs, N.J.: Prentice-Hall, 1971.

CAHN, E. S. (ed.). *Our Brother's Keeper: The Indian in White America.* New York: World (New Community Press), 1969.

CASH, JOSEPH AND HOOVER. *To Be an Indian.* New York: Holt, Rinehart & Winston, 1971.

COSTO, RUPERT. *Textbooks and the American Indian.* San Francisco: Indian Historical Press, 1970.

DAY, A. GROVE. *The Sky Clears (Poetry of the American Indians).* Lincoln: University of Nebraska, 1951.

DEBO, ANGIE. *History of the Indians of the United States.* Norman: University of Oklahoma, 1970.

DELORIA, VINE, JR. *Behind the Trail of Broken Treaties.* New York: Dell, 1974.

———. *Custer Died for Your Sins.* New York: Avon, 1970.

———. *Of Utmost Good Faith.* New York: Bantam, 1972.

———. *The Red Man in the New World Drama.* New York: Macmillan, 1971.

———. *We Talk, You Listen.* New York, Dell, 1972.

FORBES, JACK. *The Indian in America's Past.* Englewood Cliffs, N.J.: Prentice-Hall, 1964.

FUCHS, E., AND HAVIGHURST, R. *To Live on This Earth.* New York: Doubleday (Anchor), 1973.

HAMILTON, CHARLES (ed.). *Cry of the Thunderbird.* Norman: University of Oklahoma, 1972.

LEVITAN, S. A. *Big Brother's Indian Programs.* New York: McGraw-Hill, 1971.

LURIE, NANCY, AND LEVINE, STUART. *The American Indian Today,* Baltimore: Penguin (Pelican), 1968.

MARX, H. L. (ed.). *The American Indian: A Rising Ethnic Force*. New York: H. W. Wilson, 1973.

NEWCOMBE, WILLIAM W., JR. *North American Indians: An Anthropological Perspective*. Pacific Palisades, Calif.: Goodyear, 1974.

OSWALT, WENDELL H. *This Land Was Theirs: A Study of the North American Indian*. New York: John Wiley, 1966.

PRUCHA, F. P. (ed.). *Americanizing the American Indian*. Washington, D.C.: Howard University, 1973.

TURNER, FRED W. *The Portable Native American Reader*. New York: Viking, 1974.

TYLER, S. LYMAN. *A History of Indian Policy*. Washington, D.C.: U.S. Government Printing Office, 1973.

WADDELL, J., AND WATSON, M. *The American Indian in Urban Society*. Boston: Little, Brown, 1971.

WALKER, D. E., JR. *The Emergent Native American*. Boston: Little, Brown, 1972.

WASHBURN, WILCOMB. *The Indian in America*. New York: Harper & Row, 1975.

WAX, MURRAY. *Indian Americans*. Englewood Cliffs, N.J.: Prentice-Hall, 1970.

LOCATIONS PHOTOGRAPHED

INDEX